# Long-term Care Insurance

## Is it right for you?
### Are there better alternatives?

Dan Keppel, MBA
Author of *The Working Millionaire*

IAN Books

An IAN Books paperback

Published by
IAN Books
41 Watchung Plaza, B242
Montclair, NJ 07042

Cover photo: Sardinia by Robin Corps

Special sales for educational use by nonprofits.

ISBN-13: 978-1470068776
ISBN-10: 147006877X
Library of Congress Control Number: 2012902791

FREE Interactive Internet CD of the information in this book

Email your name/address to:

Support@TheInsidersGuides.com

# IAN Books at <u>Amazon.com</u>

*Wealth Without Wall Street*:
Buy Direct -- Avoid the Commissions, Fees, Loads

*The Insiders' Guides to Buying Discount Financial Services*:
Buy Direct and Save $3,000 Every Year

*Drop Your Insurance*:
Buy Only What You Need

*Create Financial Freedom Using Your* **Wealth Reserve**™:
Fix your financial life

*The Simple Financial Life*:
How to get what you want without going into debt and living
paycheck to paycheck

*Build Wealth Without Extra Money or Time*:
You don't need to budget or get an extra job

*Leah's Money Book*:
"I want to control my own money."

*The Working Millionaire*:
$2,000,000 Tax-FREE **Wealth Reserve**™ Self-insure Self-fund

*The New American Retirement System*:
a $2,000,000 Tax-FREE **Wealth Reserve**™

*Stop wasting $3,000 every year*:
101
financial products *NOT* to buy and why

*Your Retirement Spending Plan*:
Will you have enough? Where will you invest?

For savvy boomers

Sign up for our Email Alerts at
www.TheInsidersGuides.com

**New savings ideas**
**New product discounts**
**Changes in the owners of your accounts**

**Scams aimed at your money**
**Ways to avoid industry overcharges**

# Contents

**FREE savings ideas**
**Send for our**
Email Alert at
TheInsidersGuides.com/

# Introduction

## Long-term care insurance is expensive

## Insurers keep raising rates

## Almost a third of owners have to stop paying!

## Most of us will never need it

## There are better alternatives

### Do NOT buy a LTCi policy before you compare alternatives

LTCi policies average about $2,500 a year but they don't cover the full cost of care—averaging $87,235. Most sellers recommend buying before age 65 while we are still healthy and insurable but we will pay more. Like all disability insurance, we are paying for something that we may not need at all. Unlike the cost of a major medical operation covered by our comprehensive health care plan, the cost of long-term care can be estimated fairly accurately.

With a 13% and 4% chance of spending 2+ years in a nursing home for women and men respectively, the average cost will be about $200,000. If we can stay at home, a home health aide costs about $20,000 a year.

The average policy costing $2,500 a year will NOT cover all expenses. Depending on the institution we check into, daily costs are $250 a day or more. There are other medical costs— either out of pocket or a Medigap policy—that Medicare does not cover. There are other medical expenses on top of that.

Most policies do not cover our expenses from day one. Most buyers pick a 90 day "elimination" period. This means we pay a deductible of over $10,000. Most people do not buy coverage for life—three years is typical. Medicaid, a state program, picks up the cost after most of our assets are spent.

Because we are buying coverage for some period in the future—perhaps 30 years away—we must plan for inflation. Our $250 a day coverage may be worth only $120 while the price of care goes up annually. Some folks buy inflation protection with their policy but this just raises the price to perhaps $3,000 a year.

Now we may be paying $2,500 a year each for 30 years—$150,000. That is real money. Of course, if we know when we will need care exactly and/or one of us will not be around to need it, we could save premiums. However, that is usually not practical.

Bottom line—we don't want to give away $150,000 on the remote chance we might need to spend $250,000 for our care sometime in the future.

Luckily, there are alternatives.

Today you can make sure you are protected by creating a personal retirement spending plan. You need to enter the last 30 years of your life knowing how you are going to manage it. You need a realistic and flexible plan. Two-thirds of pre-retirees don't have a clue. Financial advisors favor certain products. You need less biased information to find the best alternative for you. I help you decide which alternative is best for you, now and later. Only you know what fits your lifestyle.

You have a number of alternatives. If you were lucky, your employer offered to match some of your contributions to a self-directed retirement plan (401k, etc.). Most guaranteed pensions are gone. If you were on your own, you had to figure out the most important decision about your future happiness by yourself. This was not easy but some have done it.

In recent times, most of us have had less money to build our future reserves. From 1976 to 2007, the average inflation-adjusted hourly <u>wage declined</u> by more than 7 percent. Unless you are self-employed or work a second job, you have found it hard to duplicate the guaranteed income that former generations received from their employer-paid pensions.

We have to be concerned about **having enough in retirement**. We need to know how much to spend, how much to invest and which assets to buy. I will guide you through the process. We will create a budget for a couple and a single. We can avoid income taxes as our money grows. We invest in a way that provides income for 30 years. We don't need a broker or advisor. In fact, their fees could take 40% of our money over time.

I think we all agree that, the **best guarantee of lifelong security is having money**. If we built a nest egg of $2,000,000 during our working years, we could take about $100,000 a year from the earnings without running out of money. This would cover our needs even if we had to pay for the most expensive nursing home care.

Whatever amount you have at the time of retirement is important. Even millionaires have to rely on a budget and strategic investing to make their money last as long as they do. The investment strategy you use in retirement is more important than the one you used before. It will determine how much you can spend and how long it will last.

I assume you made contributions to a retirement account at work or on your own. I assume you will have income from Social Security and perhaps a pension from an employer or two, a rollover IRA from a former pension plan, or some investments. All of these sources of income are taxable. Our first decision is to consider converting some of these into a **tax-FREE** income source in retirement.

Most advisors recommend annuities to provide a stream of payments to live on. But annuity income is taxed as regular income not tax-advantaged like capital gains, dividends or municipal bond interest. Annuities are not the best option for us.

In retirement, we want to avoid paying income taxes as long as possible. There is a new type of account, I call a **Wealth Reserve**™, that can provide tax-FREE growth AND income. This is a great strategy, especially in retirement! It uses the most powerful financial force available—**compounding** of high earnings over time. It avoids the greatest **killer** of wealth-building—TAXES. You pay no taxes on the accumulations and no taxes on the withdrawals later. And you don't pay lawyer or advisor fees either.

You let compounding work its miracle over time. You may need income for the next 30 years—65 to 95. A $100,000 deposit today can grow to $600,000 in 15 years, $1,000,000 in 20. You create your own guaranteed retirement supplement/long-term care insurance/legacy all in one fund I call a **Wealth Reserve**™. You protect both of your futures. You self-fund and self-insure your lifestyle needs in order to save the money you will need later.

I will show you how to:

1. Create a Retirement Spending system.
2. Use the best **legal** tax shelter: no taxes . . . ever.
3. Protect your family and assets with your **Wealth Reserve**™.
4. Borrow from your own 'bank' to pay for large purchases.

5. Buy whatever you need without going into debt.
6. Buy your financial services at a discount and save $3,000 a year, $75,000 over 25 years.
7. Manage your **Wealth Reserve**™ in 1 hour per year.
8. Spend according to your budgets for the rest of your lives.

You don't have to be wealthy or a financial genius to accumulate enough for your retirement needs. You just need to be a consistent investor—monthly contributions to a high growth retirement account.

If your goal is to have $250,000 (inflation-adjusted) available for future long-term care needs, then that goal guides your spending and investing habits. Do you have goals? Do they guide your spending now? If not, I will show you how to use goals.

If you have not yet built a sufficient **Wealth Reserve**™ to cover full time care, you need a **strategy**. To use assets to maintain your lifestyle now and for 30 years or more requires that you know how to invest—regularly, properly--monitor accumulations and get help when you need it. It takes only an hour to set up our Simple, Easy and Wise Plan. It takes only 1 hour per year to manage our Simple, Easy and Wise Plan. You don't pick stocks and bonds. You don't chase yield.

People who are successful preparing for retirement needs have **patience**. We have to cultivate the assets that "grow by themselves." We buy assets that grow tax-FREE. We don't buy things with credit. We **never pay interest**—we **earn** interest!

People who are successful buy only what they need. This means understanding the role of risk and reward in everyday decision-making. For instance, why pay hundreds of dollars extra for low-deductible car and home insurance when you are already self-insured by your **Wealth Reserve**™? If you carry large deductibles on all policies and accounts, you save thousands every year. You buy only what you need—catastrophic risk insurance.

I repeat: the **best guarantee of lifelong security is having money**—assets that can provide income AND provide purchasing power when you need it.

The best way to pay for long-term care when you need it may be to keep building assets before and during retirement. A **Wealth Reserve**™ can pay for *ALL* your needs—long-term care, if needed, a legacy AND wonderful retirement years. It provides "lifestyle insurance," whatever happens.

# 1

## How to pay for care in the future

In 322 B.C., Aristotle wrote:

**'Money' is a guarantee that we may have what we want in the future. Though we need nothing at the moment, it insures the possibility of satisfying a necessary desire when it arises.**

You can accumulate $250,000 for your long-term care needs. If you are lucky enough not to need it, it can be your legacy for your family. This strategy is called self-insurance. It is used by many businesses. If you are not a business owner, self-insurance is worth learning about.

We all know how little our savings grows when we put it in a bank—2% to 3%. Then, every year, we are forced to pay taxes, year after year. This is why many people don't save! The accumulation doesn't look like it is worth giving up the things they want today for wealth tomorrow. It seems like that feeling is right! The bank does NOT compound all the earnings. You must pay tax.

Range of annual returns of stocks, 1950 – 2000

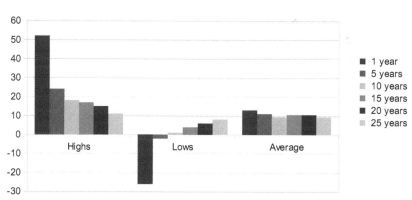

There is only one way for most of us to accumulate $600,000 from a monthly contribution: We must buy and hold the securities of growing worldwide companies AND pay **zero** tax on the growth to maximize compounding. Yes, it is more likely that investing in growing company stocks can provide more wealth than gold, real estate, or get-rich-quick schemes. In fact, over most

10-year periods, there is **no safer investment than stocks**. Since few of us can actually pick, let alone invent the next "Google," we must buy shares of a number of growing companies. If we buy a bunch using a mutual fund, we have a good chance of earning 10% to 12% per year. We can ride out the 1 out of 500 possible company failures.

      **Compounding the earnings is key**. The rich get richer— the top 1% take 23.5% of all income (up from 8.9%). And, as many millionaires have said, "the first million is the hardest." If you start with $100,000, it will take you 10 years to reach $300,000. (And only in a tax-FREE account.) However, when you have $300,000, you only have to double your money to reach $600,000. Investors in stocks, earning 11% on average, do this in about 6 years without adding new money. Plus, the wealthy have found ways to pay less tax than we do. As Warren Buffett, with $44 Thousand Millions, admitted, "I pay at a lower overall tax rate than all of my office employees." He pays only 17% **total** tax. Listen and weep: http://www.youtube.com/watch?v=Cu5B-2LoC4s.

      You can create a **Wealth Reserve**™ of $600,000 by investing $100,000 because you are compounding at 10-12% over time and you are not paying tax on the earnings. This plan also allows you to take out your contributions tax-FREE. If you let your money accumulate, you will have $600,000 for extra income AND emergencies. If you use the contributions, you need to pay it back. That is the smart way to invest. You can see how money grows in the chart on page 39. You need to understand that taking $5,000 from an account worth $250,000 is **very** different from taking $5,000 from one worth only $25,000.

      **Buy assets that "grow by themselves."** Money grows easily when you leave it alone. Its growth is stunted if you spend it or pay taxes with it. Obviously, this account grows in spurts and can go down in any year. You can actually create security (money) for yourself, but it requires time and patience. Compare your bank CD earning 2%-3%. A bank account earning 2% while the inflation rate is 3% means that you are actually losing money (security) over time. Your $100,000 deposit in the bank for 15 years will be worth about $117,000 after tax compared with about $600,000 in low-cost diversified stock funds. Of course, since there is no tax due with a **Wealth Reserve**™ when you take the money out, you will be ecstatic every April 15 (tax time).

You will have security because your ***purchasing power*** has grown over time. If you doubt that the wealthy invest in the stock market for security, take a look at the long-term returns for various Vanguard mutual funds where they put their money. Some of these funds have provided investors with $2,000,000 or more for their retirement.

You might take a "loan" from your **Wealth Reserve**™ to buy your first home or for living expenses if you become disabled. Think of the security you have as you go through life. The **Wealth Reserve**™ that you have might launch you in a business or make sure your kids go to college. When you understand how your **Wealth Reserve**™ works, you will pay back the "loan" so you have the Reserve for another time. This is the lesson that the wealthy have learned generation after generation. You earn 10% to 12% on your money. You could buy all ten Vanguard funds and receive 11.8% total return with less risk. When one fund is down, others are up.

| 2011 Total Return | Fund | Long-term Return* | Longevity |
|---|---|---|---|
| 1.97% | 500 Index | 10.36% | since 1976 |
| -1.74% | Energy | 12.71% | since 1984 |
| -3.73% | Extended Market | 9.96% | since 1987 |
| 11.45% | Health | 16.30% | since 1984 |
| -13.68% | International Growth | 10.50% | since 1981 |
| -1.84% | PRIMECAP | 12.79% | since 1984 |
| -2.80% | Small Cap Index | 10.26% | since 1960 |
| 9.63% | Wellesley Income | 10.16% | since 1970 |
| -4.00% | Windsor | 11.00% | since 1958 |
| 2.70% | Windsor II | 10.18% | since 1985 |
| 0.00% | Average | 11.42% | |

*Average Annual Returns as of 12/31/11.

That kind of security begins with your commitment to a regular contribution ... and patience. TIME will work magic on your **Wealth Reserve**™ fund. I was inspired by the patience of Susan and Fred, friends from work. Their financial plan was the inspiration for the "**Wealth Reserve**™." Here is their story: "Fred and Susan had a baby—Natalie—in 1975. They lived in lower Manhattan and I knew them because Susan worked with me sometimes. It began when we started talking about the baby. Susan asked me what to do with the money they received from relatives and friends for Natalie's birth. They wanted to protect their new child's future and to have college money. Both of them had good insurance benefits at work. I suggested that Susan and Fred look at individual stocks."

## Susan and Fred's 'college' fund

| Market Returns | Account Value | | Natalie | Year | |
|---|---|---|---|---|---|
| | $5,000 | Natalie | | | |
| 37% | $12,604 | | 0 | 1975 | |
| 24% | $20,837 | | 1 | 1976 | |
| -8% | $23,034 | | 2 | 1977 | |
| 6% | $28,868 | | 3 | 1978 | |
| | | | | | Paid $1,000 to repair car |
| 18% | $38,020 | | 4 | 1979 | |
| 32% | $55,731 | | 5 | 1980 | |
| -5% | $56,934 | | 6 | 1981 | |
| 22% | $74,584 | | 7 | 1982 | |
| 21% | $95,328 | | 8 | 1983 | |
| 6% | $105,500 | | 9 | 1984 | |
| | | | | | Paid $15000 for house |
| 32% | $129,804 | | 10 | 1985 | |
| 19% | $159,465 | | 11 | 1986 | |
| 5% | $171,848 | | 12 | 1987 | |
| 17% | $205,976 | | 13 | 1988 | |
| 32% | $277,433 | | 14 | 1989 | |
| -3% | $273,184 | | 15 | 1990 | |
| 31% | $363,373 | | 16 | 1991 | |
| 8% | $396,979 | | 17 | 1992 | |
| 10% | $441,296 | | 18 | 1993 | |
| 2% | $454,406 | | 19 | 1994 | |
| | | | | | Susan disabled-stop $350/mo |
| 38% | $632,877 | | 20 | 1995 | Paid $6,300 for vacation |
| 23% | $772,138 | | 21 | 1996 | Paid $56,350 for loans and tax |
| 33% | $970,594 | | 22 | 1997 | Paid $10,000 for roof repair |
| 28% | $1,232,360 | | 23 | 1998 | |
| 21% | $1,491,156 | | 24 | 1999 | |
| -9% | $1,356,952 | | 25 | 2000 | |
| -12% | $1,195,475 | | 26 | 2001 | |
| -22% | $931,275 | | 27 | 2002 | |
| 29% | $1,201,344 | | 28 | 2003 | |
| 11% | $1,333,492 | | 29 | 2004 | |
| 5% | $1,400,167 | | 30 | 2005 | |
| 16% | $1,624,194 | | 31 | 2006 | |

*They contributed $350 per month or $4,200 per year to "college" fund. Inflation adjusted dollars.

"They talked it over and agreed. They asked me what stocks to buy and why. I told them they could pick any stock in the Dow. They picked the ones with the highest yield and the lowest price. Susan is bright. She was an underwriter. This was in 1975 or '76. I forget which ones they purchased—ATT, Johnson & Johnson, GE, GM—you know, the household names."

"They agreed on buying stocks because they could buy them directly from the companies and hold them without paying tax on the increased value until they needed the money. Dividends were reinvested and the income tax on the earnings was not outrageous. These plans are now called DSP and DRIPS. Susan and Fred called these accounts their "college fund." I think they had $5,000 from gifts and they contributed $350 a month ($6 a day) plus extra income from time to time. Most of the companies they picked allowed them to buy stocks without a broker's fee. By the time Natalie was 18, Fred and Susan had about $300,000."

"They kept putting money in each month. During the bad years—you know 1977-78, they had second thoughts. But Susan kept them on track."

"They had a car accident a few years after they started and needed money to pay for the policy deductible. They were saving about $200 a year by taking the $1,000 deductible. So they needed to sell $1,000 of stock. They sold stock that was down that year. In fact, I think they did not have to pay any tax on that sale. Anyway, that $1,000 sale did not hurt them. They still ended up with about $300,000. And remember, all this time—18 years—they have saved $200 on their car insurance. That's $3,600 of the $75,600 ($350 X 12 mo. X 18 yrs.) they invested."

"Like most families, they wanted a house. They got tired of paying rent and needed a good place for Natalie to go to school. The cost of the down payment—$15,000—came from Natalie's college fund. They still ended up with about $300,000. But what they found was that some of the stocks had done worse than others. They sold the worst ones, paying little tax on the gain. They found that most of the $15,000 withdrawal was money they had already paid tax on. They paid the capital gains tax of 20% on about $5,000 of the $15,000. That was the profit on the stock they sold."

"They usually receive a tax refund because they both worked, so that year it was smaller. That was all that happened. They purchased the house with the $15,000 and avoided the mortgage insurance that bankers usually charge those who have less than a 20% down payment. This saved them more money each year too."

"In a sense then, part of the $350 they paid each month for the college fund was actually paid for by the savings from the fact they had enough of a down payment not to need private mortgage insurance. They saved on their homeowners by picking a $5,000 deductible and not needing expensive extras, like coverage for jewelry or furs. They saved on credit life, disability, unemployment, and PMI insurance that the mortgage bank tried to add to their mortgage payment. All these helped pay for the college fund."

> Their "College" Fund became a **WEALTH RESERVE**

"No one explains these options when you are starting out. The agent wants to pile on more premiums to raise the commission. The banker wants to pile on higher mortgage fees. The lawyer doesn't get paid to save you money. Your parents help you as much as they can. Susan and Fred were lucky. They got the help they needed early, but everyone can do the same kind of saving today.

"In order to protect the $300,000 fund and all their other assets, Fred found out about umbrella liability insurance. For $210 a year, Susan and Fred would have $1,000,000 coverage in case they were sued and needed to pay a lawyer to defend themselves. Even if the accident was their fault, the policy covered the judgment and the lawyer fees too."

"They were finally ready for Natalie to go to college. They had $300,000 available for her when she was 18 years old. Of course she didn't need the money all at once. And when she made her decision about where to go to college she chose a very good state college that cost only $10,000 a year."

"During this time educational loans were very cheap. So Fred and Susan decided to let the college fund grow—20% to 25% a year— during the 90's. They knew this was unusual because the average gain for Dow stocks was 12% a year. They let the loans grow for the first two years until they could see that they had earned $60,000 for two years straight. We discussed this and decided this couldn't last. So they sold enough stock to pay the loans and the tax on the stock earnings. Now they realized they did not have to worry about the college loans any more."

"Susan told me right before she took another job that they had easily taken care of Natalie's college expense each year from the college fund. They stopped paying for life insurance policies that she and Fred owned. This saved them another $2,500 a year and they continued to invest the $350 per month. It was getting easier with fewer expenses. As a backup emergency fund, they took out a home equity line of credit that cost them nothing—no fees or closing costs. They would pay the loan market rate only *if* they needed to use the line for emergencies."

"One thing they did not anticipate: Susan was disabled within the year. She no longer had disability insurance from work. She was not able to work at all. They decided to cut back on their entertainment, vacation, and hobbies in order to get by on Fred's salary. They also had an emergency expense. They had to sell stock to pay $10,000 for Fred's parent's home repair. The tax on the earnings of the stocks did not push them into the next tax bracket, so they are actually paying much less tax this year anyway. Susan got better and they were able to give Natalie a fabulous graduation party and trip to California as a present."

"The next year after Natalie graduated; Susan and Fred decided to start their own business. Fred would work part-time. Susan would work full-time in what she loved—framing people's pictures. Fred would do the woodwork. Susan would run the store in a charming village nearby. The college fund—now $600,000 or so— gave them the feeling that they would have incomes until they got the store into the black. They paid the store's rent and utilities. The store liability policy was not too bad after Susan picked a higher deductible. Fred's job would provide the health insurance they needed."

> **WEALTH RESERVE** also used to self-insure some risks.

    "The store business allows Fred and Susan to deduct many of the normal expenses associated with their activities. The 'college' fund, no longer for college, allowed them to save more on the protection they need for retirement. They attended a seminar on long term care insurance and decided that they could afford it but didn't need it. According to page 6 of the *Shopper's Guide* they received at the seminar, the chance of Fred needing expensive care was 4%; Susan 13%."

    "If they spent $4,000 a year for up to 30 years, they might never get to use that $120,000 [$2,000 each, times 30 years] because they both were in good health. Besides, 25% of LTCi buyers drop it within two years. So, Fred and Susan put the $4,000 in their tax-advantaged retirement plan, connected with their business. This will add another $600,000 for any emergency, including remodeling their home for easy access and hiring a home health aide. These are the most common needs people have, according to the booklet. Worst case, they use the assets in the business which helps them with health care."

"Fred was still a teacher working part-time and Susan loves the way a picture looks—even bad ones—in a frame."


## How the **Wealth Reserve**™ works

The **Wealth Reserve**™ is actually a Roth IRA account—the IRS's own tax haven for the working person! The rules are pretty simple —taxed money goes in and tax-FREE earnings come out after age 59 ½. Take your contributions out anytime.

Contributions are limited to $5,000 (2012), but may rise in future years. http://www.irs.gov/publications/p590/ch02.html There are income limits but most people don't hit the earnings limit of $125,000 (2012). If you are married, the limit is $183,000 (2012). You make your deposit to your **Wealth Reserve**™ automatic so you can't forget to do it each month.

You may also invest in your employer's Roth 401k if your employer matches it. You don't reduce your income tax with these contributions. However, they grow tax FREE forever. You can contribute up to $17,000 (2012). If your employer matches your funds, it really boosts your 401k growth. It's free money. You will have tax-FREE income from both accounts later.

Of course you can make contributions to your Roth 401k if your employer offers it in the retirement plan. Many young people prefer to be taxed at the beginning of their careers since their salaries do not draw high tax rates yet. The contribution limit may be raised. See irs.gov/retirement/article/0,,id=152956,00.html#5.

There are no limits on an employee's income in determining if he or she can make designated Roth 401(k) contributions. Of course, the employer has to offer Roth 401(k) deferrals. If you decide to invest $10,000 a year for 10 years in a stock market index inside their employer's Roth 401k plan, you could accumulate $180,000 with NO federal income taxation to pay on the earnings. The tax savings might be worth an extra 25% since all taxes are avoided.

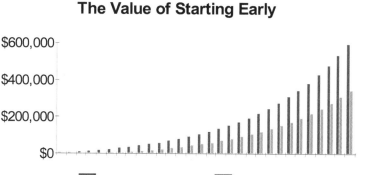

## The Value of Starting Early

You can open your account at any age as long as you have *earned* income. Stock dividends or interest do not count. Any job will do. You don't even need a job requiring a W-2 to prove it. A part-time, weekend or night job will do. Any cash-only work will also qualify. Accountants recommend that receipts and records be maintained. You could even work for yourself in a home-office business.

Your contributions to the account should not pass through your hands. You should have the money taken directly from your bank account by the IRA trustee. For all distributions to be tax-FREE, a Roth IRA must have existed for at least five years before the distribution. Contributions are after-tax so you can take them, if necessary, with no tax payable. Nontaxable distributions from a Roth IRA won't affect your eligibility for student aid either. Later, in retirement, this money won't effect your social security benefits as of the rules today.

Alternatively, if you already have a Roth IRA with significant values, you can use it to do your gift and estate planning. You don't have to take the money out beginning at age 70½, unlike the regular IRA. You can let it grow. You can name your grandchild beneficiary which will be effective for both property law and income tax purposes. Obviously, as beneficiary, your grandchild could just liquidate the account and thus lose the value for their "Gift of a Lifetime." If you fear this could happen, you could name your child or you might need to establish a trust to control the distributions. See your lawyer.

A person who inherits a Roth—unlike the original owner of the account—is required to withdraw a percentage of the funds annually, based on their age. The younger the person when they inherit, the longer they can stretch out those withdrawals, enjoying more time for potential tax-free growth of the investments. That means that your inheritance could get bigger as they get older. Each year, the required distributions from the Roth, divided into separate inherited accounts, would be calculated based on each grandchild's age and might go into his or her individual trust. You could have the mandatory distributions paid to the child's parent or other custodian until the child is of a responsible age. The trust has to be worded so that it precisely follows some "tricky" IRS rules, so make sure you work with an attorney who has extensive experience setting these up. A $100,000 inherited Roth IRA could be worth $2-3 millions over their lifetimes. http://www.fairmark.com/rothira/inherit.htm

If you own a Roth IRA, you can split it into equal shares and name each grandchild as primary beneficiary. While the Roth IRAs will be included in your taxable estate and so be subject to federal estate tax, the Roth IRA will pass to the grandchild and could be tax free. This is not tax advice. See your lawyer.

Your grandchildren can avoid the 10% early distribution penalty and withdraw earnings tax-FREE even if they are under age 59½. They inherited the money. Usually the grandchild can take distributions over their entire life span—reducing the amount and allowing the bulk of the inheritance to grow tax-FREE. Ask your accountant for details.

The Roth IRA is NOT the best way for you to save for your kid's college expenses. You can own a 529 college savings plan for the benefit of your child. You can contribute more money to a 529 than to a Roth IRA. Grandparents can lower their estate tax by contributing. You can change beneficiaries if your child does not want to go to college. You can use it yourself. You don't give up control of the funds. And if started early enough, 18 years is enough time to accumulate completely tax-FREE funds (including earnings) for education expenses. Find our Insiders Guide to Education Funding through TheInsidersGuides.com

The Roth IRA allows you take "qualified" withdrawals—for your 1st home and disability—which are not included as taxable income, unlike other savings plans—savings bonds, mutual funds, etc. You benefit through lower income taxes by putting money in a tax-free investment versus paying taxes on dividends each year in a taxable savings or investment account.

**The miracle of compounding and tax-FREE growth**

**Tax-FREE v Taxable**

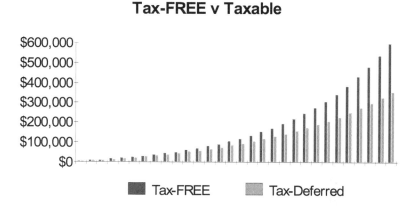

Ben Franklin was wrong about death and taxes! Taxes can be avoided. The point of your contributions to a Roth IRA is that the growth of the contributions is NOT TAXED as it grows and NOT TAXED as it comes out of the account.

## No other investment vehicle is like that.

Your **Wealth Reserve**™ balloons to $500,000 because 1) it grows without taxation, and 2) time allows interest to be earned on interest and earnings on earnings. The account grows in **geometric progression**. The top lines in the graph below is measured on a larger scale than the bottom ones. Since the money is invested in stocks over a long period of time, it can compound at 10% or more annually, assuming you don't take it out.

Using both of these factors creates a balance that really *sings*. Taken individually by themselves, your monthly contributions of any amount might not impress you. However, the element of time and tax-FREE earnings really gets your attention over the years. This is how wealth is created. A wealthy person works the same number of days as you do. However, when their wealth works day and night too, the accumulation line (top lines) can literally go off the chart. In most 10-year periods, losses are recovered.

# Cumulative Wealth

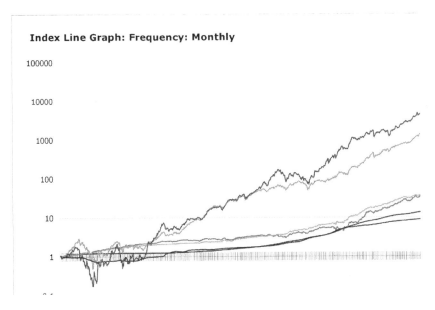

Top line—Small Cap Stocks
2nd line—Large Cap Stocks (S&P 500)
3rd line—US Long-term Corporate Bonds
4th line—Intermediate-term Government Bonds
5th line—US 30 day Government T-bills
6th line—US inflation

Courtesy: Dr. Campbell R. Harvey http://www.duke.edu/~charvey/

Historically, wealth doubles in value every 8-10 years if left alone. Of course the stock market doesn't move up at 10% every year. However, the **Wealth Reserve**™ will double and double and double so that by age 65, you could have over $2 million. Notice how the account values in the graph on page 39 move from $1 million to $2 million in 9 years, even with 3 years of losses. Of course, a million dollars will be worth less in the future because of inflation. But you will certainly appreciate your account later no matter what your contributions are now.

And the bonus of this geometric account growth is that it does not quit even after you stop adding your monthly contributions. Once the account has reached a certain mass, let's say after 30 years of contributions or $90,000, it will keep compounding. On page 39 we show you how this can work for contributions to a

**Wealth Reserve**™ invested in an actual U.S. stock index fund (500 Index) over time.

You can see in the chart "Cumulative Wealth" above that over time, wealth accumulates at different rates depending on the type of assets you buy. For anyone who invested in smaller companies over any given 15 year period, the benefits were outstanding. For each $1,000 invested in 1940, $3,000,000 was the total return by the 1990's. Investing more cautiously, in the large companies of the S&P 500, for instance, your $1,000 would have grown to almost a $1,000,00 by 2000. Yes, the lines are not perfectly straight, but growing $250 a month to $2,000,000 is definitely worth the ups and downs. Inflation is designated by the bottom line here. Putting all your money in a bank CD would accumulate at a rate represented by a line near that bottom line.

You can see that the **best gift you can give to yourself** is a **Wealth Reserve**™ invested in a group of stocks over a long period of time. A low-cost index fund like the Vanguard Total Stock Index provides the best chance of maximizing earnings as the market leaders change over time. It won't matter which style or sector is rising or falling at any given time. The account owns them all and thus you benefit over the long haul. Since stocks have averaged about 10% over time and an index costs only 0.07% ($7 per $10,000), your account compounds at 10% or more versus 8.5% for funds paying managers with expensive bonuses. According to a Morningstar study:

**"In every single time period and data point tested, low-cost funds beat high-cost funds."**
personal.vanguard.com/pdf/morningstar.pdf

You can understand how this account works. If you don't stop contributing or take money out when the account goes down temporarily, you will have money for retirement. Learn patience. TIME is the key ingredient in this formula. Success does not require stock trading. Get rich quick schemes only work for the seller. This plan does not require working longer hours. It does not require checking your account every day. **It requires just waiting** for compounding to work. And sometimes that is hard to do. When others panic, you must be steady. Start it and forget it.

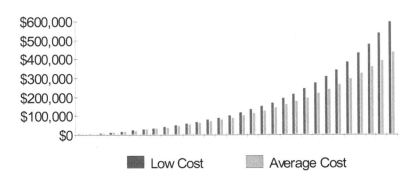

**Cost Matters: 0.19% v 1.68%**

Low Cost    Average Cost

## How to get started

All you have to do is open the account online or by phone, provide a bank account number to the trustee and sign the paperwork. Do it and forget it. You don't need a broker or advisor. Just do it. It is your gift to yourself—**The GIFT OF A LIFETIME**.

Let's say you don't have $250 a month. Of course, you can invest whatever you want. But you want to help yourself as much as possible. You can use our *Guides* to uncover savings in your current spending that can provide money for your contributions. You can use our *Guides* to find extra money to grow your **Wealth Reserve**™ for your future.

For instance, you could save $600 or more just by changing your deductible on your auto or home insurance. Learn the insider tricks of buying auto and home coverage and save. See **Insider's Guides to Vehicle** and **Home Insurance** below. You might drop some of the coverage you don't need. like credit or permanent life insurance. Check our **Insider's Guide to Buying Life Insurance**. You could save big by transferring your mutual funds to a low-cost provider like Vanguard, TIAA-CREF or Fidelity. Some clients have saved $3,000 a year just with this one change. You will discover that no money manager can be right all the time. Market index funds beat 86% of all managed mutual funds. businessweek.com/investing/insights/blog/archives/2009/04/ Use our **Insider's Guide to Buying Mutual Funds & Securities.**

In fact you should start by reading the chapter called, **12 Things your Agent, Broker, Banker, Money Manager ... Will**

**NOT Tell You**. If you are like most people, you want to save on the things you really don't need but you don't know which financial products are best or where to buy them. Many people can save $3,000 a year without changing their lifestyle. Often, it is just a matter of recognizing that we have changed but our old obligations have not. We don't examine our habits. For instance, some people find their cable bill has escalated and they really don't need a package they still have. Others don't realize they don't need life and disability insurance in their auto policy. The routines of daily life don't let us question our assumptions periodically. Family needs and lifestyles change. We become involved in different activities. We just don't question what we spend money on.

You can also help yourself by using our *Guides* when you need any financial product. When it comes time to buy a mortgage or invest for college, let our *Guides* help you decide which account is best. You could save on banking and auto purchases. Our *Guide* offers insider advice from those that work in these industries.

> A **WEALTH RESERVE** provides tax-FREE income

Our *Guides* show you how to buy only what you need, not what provides the highest profit to the sellers. After working in the financial services business for 20 years— brokerage, banks, advisory firm—I can assure you that the retail products offered to the public are created and chosen for the benefit of the sellers not the end user—you. This industry has changed dramatically. Now you can buy and sell stocks for zero commission, invest in a mutual fund for fees of 0.01%, buy term life insurance directly from the manufacturer. You can buy almost all financial products at substantial discounts from the products sold by the industry middle-people. The products are usually better too.

So you can help yourself by building your **Wealth Reserve**™ of $2 million AND finding how and where to save on all your financial needs. Take advantage of these savings too. Add them to your Reserve: See the list of savings below. The *Guides* are now available in one volume at TheInsidersGuides.com.

Now you have a plan to build a **Wealth Reserve**™. It can serve as your **emergency** fund, your **self-insurance** fund, your **loan** fund, and your **retirement** system. Over your lifetime, you have a way to meet your needs without wasting money on taxes, fees and interest paid to others. You are using your money to buy assets that "grow by themselves." Your money pays *you* interest instead of you paying interest to others. Your account compounds capital gains on capital gains. None of it is used to pay taxes.

You have the **new financial system**. It doesn't matter what happens to Social Security or your company's pension plan. You are not relying on the government or others to pay or not pay toward your bountiful lifestyle.

## Your **Wealth Reserve**™ is your new financial system

| Monthly | Accumulation at 12% per year | | | | | | | | | |
|---|---|---|---|---|---|---|---|---|---|---|
| | 5 | 10 | 15 | 20 | 25 | 30 | 35 | 40 | 45 | 50 |
| $100 | $8,167 | $23,004 | $49,958 | $98,925 | $187,884 | $349,496 | $643,095 | $1,176,477 | $2,145,469 | $3,905,834 |
| $200 | $16,334 | $46,008 | $99,916 | $197,850 | $375,768 | $698,992 | $1,286,190 | $2,352,954 | $4,290,938 | $7,811,668 |
| $300 | $24,501 | $69,012 | $149,874 | $296,775 | $563,652 | $1,048,488 | $1,929,285 | $3,529,431 | $6,436,408 | $11,717,502 |
| $500 | $40,835 | $115,020 | $249,790 | $494,625 | $939,420 | $1,747,480 | $3,215,475 | $5,882,385 | $10,727,346 | $19,529,169 |

# 2

## A Simple, Easy and Wise Plan

People who are successful have a plan.

If you want to have a guaranteed income from a new tax-FREE $600,000 **Wealth Reserve**™, you need a way to make it happen. To be able to have an additional $600,000 from $100,000 requires that you know how to invest properly and get help when you need it. It takes only one hour to set up the Simple, Easy and Wise Plan and only 1 hour per year to manage it.

Picking *individual* stocks as a strategy is not likely to work for you. Warren Buffett is probably history's greatest investor, in terms of results with $44B ($44 thousand million dollars) so far. He buys *companies* that provide valuable services to a great number of people. His company owns parts of Coke, GEICO, Fruit of the Loom, Benjamin Moore, Acme Bricks, etc. berkshirehathaway.com/ He told Reuters: "A very low-cost index is going to beat a majority of the amateur-managed money or professionally-managed money." Many studies have shown that low-cost index funds beat 86% of funds with a stock picking manager. *BusinessWeek* Apr 2009. A February 2009 study provides more evidence that investing in simple, low-cost **index funds** often leads to better net returns. Compare the odds of selecting the correct mutual fund. Your fund's chance of beating the market in EACH year is 3 out of 100. nytimes.com/2009/02/22/your-money/stocks-and-bonds/22stra.html

Other studies have shown that successful investing is a result of owning quality stocks or stock mutual funds **over a long period of time**. Most people are not patient so they are not successful investors. You can build wealth by owning the stocks of profitable businesses over time. Anne Scheiber did it by herself and left $20 million to her favorite charity, money.cnn.com/magazines/moneymag/moneymag_archive/1996/01/01/207651/index.

I have helped people who have never reached their goal because they have not learned what it takes to get there. They started saving but they did not learn about the **miracle of**

**compounding.** They saved in their bank at 2% or 3% interest rate. They became frustrated because they only had $18,000 after three years of saving $500 a month. So they quit saving and bought a SuperCrew 145 XLT for $637 a month for 60 months. They did not know that they could have earned over $50,000 by investing that same amount of money in a low-cost stock mutual fund.

Most people never learn how compounding of earnings works. In short, we never learn that every $100 is worth $10,000 to us in time if we invest in companies that share their profits with us. A stock index fund helps you earn an average of 12% per year without losing all your money if one company fails. You cannot become financially independent without investing in profitable companies. Compare your actual returns from bank CDs to stocks. At 3%, your $250 monthly contribution to a CDs earns $200,000 in 37 years. At 12%, your **Wealth Reserve**™ would have about $2 million from stocks. Which do you want?

## A Simple, Easy, Wise Strategy

My strategy incorporates a unique technique to assure that you reach your goal: a **Wealth Reserve**™. People spend more time planning a vacation than their financial future. You can use a simple, easy and wise strategy to insure yourself of a healthy financial life. Consistency wins. You create a **Wealth Reserve**™ as Step 1.

| Start |
| :---: |
| your |
| **WEALTH** |
| **RESERVE**™ |
| in |
| three steps |

Step **1**. Build your **Wealth Reserve**™. Your **Wealth Reserve**™ consists of mutual funds inside the Roth IRA trust account. The account grows without taxation on the earnings. You may also invest through a retirement plan Roth 401k at work. Since few companies are offering a paid pension, most independents are making the investment decisions on their own. A **Wealth Reserve**™ refers to the fact that it can also be used to insure some of your risks. You are relieved of the need to waste money on some insurance policies. You are building a reserve against a possible loss and creating more Wealth at the same time. The Reserve may serve two purposes—a Reserve for unforeseen contingencies and a fund that makes loans and later provides

28

income to supplement a modified Social Security.

A great example of this is the risk of premature death. With a term policy for 10 years at a time, you can replace lost family income if you are not around. You can buy a 10 year term policy for about a $1 a day even at age 50. If you have built your **Wealth Reserve**™ over time, your family will have a **Wealth Reserve**™ of much more than a permanent life insurance benefit can possibly provide.

Before easy access to mutual funds, life insurance was considered an investment. If you paid $2,000 a year in premiums for 50 years, your family would receive a benefit of $300,000 at your death! Today, you and your family can enjoy $2 million for any lifestyle need! You can obtain term to cover your family for $1 a day during your working years. It is cheap because the risk is low. Your **Wealth Reserve**™ is there for you in case you are disabled or your Social Security is reduced. Your family will have money to make the transition if you are not around.

During your working life, you will earn about $2.5 to $3 million before taxes. If you invest **just** 10 percent of that income, you can accumulate another $2 million to accomplish all that you want to do in life. Your **Wealth Reserve**™ assures you of having enough no matter what happens. I assume that you will not spend every cent that you earn. However, if you start investing early, you will provide the reserve of $2 million when you need it. Investing is really about TIME. Consider what could happen if you invest $100 a month at the birth of your grandchild. Their **Wealth Reserve**™ might be $125,000 by age 18, depending on the asset you bought. They might have $1 million by age 40.

## How assets build the **Wealth Reserve**™

| Monthly Accumulation at 12% per year | | | | | | | | | |
|---|---|---|---|---|---|---|---|---|---|
| | 5 | 10 | 15 | 20 | 25 | 30 | 35 | 40 | 45 | 50 |
| $100 | $8,167 | $23,004 | $49,958 | $98,925 | $187,884 | $349,496 | $643,095 | $1,176,477 | $2,145,469 | $3,905,834 |
| $200 | $16,334 | $46,008 | $99,916 | $197,850 | $375,768 | $698,992 | $1,286,190 | $2,352,954 | $4,290,938 | $7,811,668 |
| $300 | $24,501 | $69,012 | $149,874 | $296,775 | $563,652 | $1,048,488 | $1,929,285 | $3,529,431 | $6,436,408 | $11,717,502 |
| $500 | $40,835 | $115,020 | $249,790 | $494,625 | $939,420 | $1,747,480 | $3,215,475 | $5,882,385 | $10,727,346 | $19,529,169 |

## It is never too late. Start today

Step **2**. The *amount of time* you have to accomplish your income goal determines the type of investment you need. Even though we can't predict the day, month and year of ups and downs, the stock market goes up about <u>10-12% a year</u>, over most 10-year periods. These Vanguard mutual funds have earned over 10% for a long time. Of course, there is no guarantee of future returns:

| 2010 Total Return | Fund | Long-term Return | Longevity |
|---|---|---|---|
| 14.9% | 500 Index | 10.6%* | since 1976 |
| 13.4% | Energy | 13.3% | since 1984 |
| 27.4% | Extended Market | 10.6% | since 1987 |
| 6.2% | Health | 16.6% | since 1984 |
| 15.7% | International Growth | 11.4% | since 1981 |
| 12.9% | PRIMECAP | 13.4% | since 1984 |
| 27.7% | Small Cap Index | 10.5% | since 1960 |
| 10.7% | Wellesley Income | 10.2% | since 1970 |
| 14.8% | Windsor | 11.3% | since 1958 |
| 10.6% | Windsor II | 10.5% | since 1985 |
| 15.4% | Average | 11.8% | |

*Average Annual Returns as of 12/31/10.

Most pension funds are invested in stocks and bonds. Even though the market fell 22% in 2002 and jumped 29% in 2003, the average was still holding. See page 39. And, with a Roth IRA, your money can compound tax-FREE, providing an extra 25% when you take it out. You never pay income tax.

## Accumulation 1990-2010 Market Returns

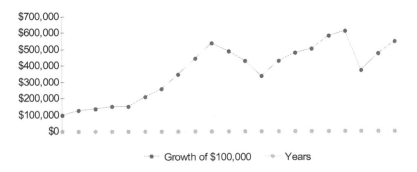

It matters how much money you start investing when you start late. The **key to reaching any money goal is TIME**—not luck or skill —TIME to let the power of compounding work its magic to turn $100,000 into $600,000 over time. Unfortunately, most people will need that $600,000 later as our life expectancies grow to 90 years.

You can build a $600,000 fund for income in 20 years. You need to invest $100,000 in low-cost stock mutual funds. Since the Roth IRA contribution limit is now $5,000, you may only be able to achieve your goal by converting your IRA or rollover IRA (401k) to a Roth. moneychimp.com/articles/rothira/contribution_limits.htm

Step 3. **Start NOW**. It's never too late. Buy one or all 10 of the funds listed above. They are assets that *grow by themselves*. Convert as much of your IRA as you can afford in taxes each year. If you have earned income, you and your spouse might afford $6,000 a year to help reach your goal for later years. If you are doing your estate planning, you can give the Gift of a Lifetime to your grandchildren: just $10,000 invested by age 20 can become $2 million by age 65.
moneychimp.com/calculator/compound_interest_calculator.htm

Most successful people let TIME do the work. As Warren Buffett, the world's best investor, said, "We continue to make more money when *snoring* than when active." Berkshirehathaway.com/

If your goal is to provide a college education, you can invest just $3.33 a day for 18 years and give about $90,000. If you invest another $3.33 a day for 39 years, they could have over $1 million for their retirement. And using a ROTH IRA makes it tax-FREE. fairmark.com/rothira/contrib.htm

My clients implement their strategy by calling one of the low-cost mutual funds like Vanguard, Fidelity or TIAA-CREF and opening a Roth IRA account. Others did it online. These firms provide the best value for your money since their fees are low.

Since they completed the application themselves, they saved 5.75% of their money on commissions (loads). Vanguard.com and TIAA-CREF.org are run for your benefit—not the managers—so their annual fees are very low—at cost.

You can request a ROTH IRA application by phone. You may have a tax penalty if use all of it before age 60. Exceptions: first home and disability See RothIRA.com. Compounding without current taxes supercharges your **Wealth Reserve**™. If you already have a Roth IRA, you can fund your spouse's, child's or grandchild's.

A ROTH IRA allows you to grow the assets without tax ... ever —it's FREE of federal income tax as long as they keep it open for five years and withdraw earnings after age 59½, except for paying for their first home and disability income. Also, you may receive a tax <u>CREDIT</u> for $1,000 for the ROTH IRA (2010).

Request a prospectus (owner's manual) for each fund you will be using. Most clients favor low-cost. Your **Wealth Reserve**™ is a long-term investment, so buy one or more of the Vanguard funds above. Other low-cost funds are provided by <u>TIAA-CREF Equity Index</u> or the Fidelity Spartan. The Vanguard 500 has very large American companies. Some clients add <u>International Stock</u> or TIAA <u>International Equity</u> since they represent markets around the world. The Energy and Health funds already have global giants.

Keep it simple by buying all the funds from one company. You will receive only one statement with the fund's returns listed.

The account application allows you to begin an automatic monthly debit from your checking account. This assures that you pay the <u>lowest share cost</u>. There is a section for Roth IRA beneficiaries. Most people list their spouse as primary and children as contingent. The telephone representatives can answer any specific fund questions you have.

This strategy provides you with the **best chance of accumulating** the greatest amount with the least risk over time while not wasting a dime of your money on a high paid manager. You may use a Roth 401k at work. That Roth <u>401k</u> works the same way but you can contribute much more to it.
irs.gov/retirement/article/0,,id=152956,00.html.

**The Simple Financial Life** strategy provides you with diversification and "<u>dollar cost averaging</u>," the lowest-cost method (<u>investopedia.com</u>) of buying the companies you may use everyday. Pensions, insurers, and trusts invest in the market using low-cost funds just like you can. An advisor is not necessary since you are not interested in chasing last year's hot mutual fund. The expenses are as low as $7 per $10,000 vs. $134 every year for the average stock fund manager's high salary.


## Why use funds from Vanguard or TIAA-CREF?

Did you know that most Wall Street insiders do not follow the advice of retail brokers or the popular financial press. They invest most of their serious money in low-cost funds or shares of index funds (ETFs) because they realize excessive costs lower the returns of most fund managers over 10 years, especially in down markets.

There are many books written on the subject of index

versus "managed" funds. If you wish to vanquish the hype and understand investing, skim *A Random Walk Down Wall Street* by Princeton University's Burton Malkiel. Here are the reasons why smart insiders use low-cost funds:

1. Both stock and bond index funds provide better returns than 86% of managed funds for periods greater than 10 years.
2. You earn more because you pay lower costs and taxes.
3. Low-cost funds build greater wealth over time.
4. Low-cost funds can be less volatile because they reflect whole sectors of the market.
5. Low-cost funds offer better diversification.
6. You know what you are paying for. No high-salary managers.
7. Low-cost funds don't require you to hope the manager will predict the future correctly. The odds of doing it are 1 in 15,000 each year separately. Over time, all funds provide average returns minus their costs.
8. Low-cost funds are easy to buy.

> "Professional money management is a gigantic rip-off."
> Bill Gross, star bond manager, *Everything You've Heard About Investing is Wrong*

## This is a summary of many studies about investing

**First**, fund managers try to predict the future of the market when they buy and sell securities in their funds. There is no proof this can be done well over time. Yesterday's winners are usually tomorrow's losers. The AVERAGE market return has been 12%, so a few managers will beat the average by luck—Just not the same ones every year. nytimes.com/2008/07/13/business/13stra.html
**Second**, the costs of the manager, their staff and operations must be paid for by you whether or not they earn you a dime. It is always better to pay as little as possible for the same performance. Costs can take 33% of your returns over time. Surprisingly, while the stock index rose 9%, investors with high paid managers averaged only 2.56% annually from 1990-2010 (QAIB). DALBARinc.com.
**Third**, high cost managers get paid for increasing the size of their funds, not for making you rich. Bringing in more money is a full-

time job. It is expensive to market the funds given that there are now thousands available. It is inevitable that popular funds will grow until they produce average returns with high expenses. Managers want to be rich, not right.

**Fourth**, there is much less chance of you being treated poorly by fund management if the structure and governance are customer-oriented like Vanguard's and TIAA-CREF's are.

**Fifth**, many professional managers and Wall Street insiders place their core assets in low-cost index funds.

## Here are some of their statements:

Warren Buffett, the most successful investor
"Most investors, both institutional and individual, will find that the best way to own common stocks is through an index fund that charges minimal fees.... Paradoxically, when 'dumb' money acknowledges its limitations, it ceases to be dumb." Berkshirehathaway.com/letters/1993.html.

Peter Lynch, brilliant manager, Magellan Fund "...you'd be just as well off if you'd invested in the S&P 500." *One Up on Wall Street*, 1989, p. 240.

Jonathan Clements, formerly *The Wall Street Journal*
"Most people can do it themselves. ... By indexing, you don't just ensure that you will do better than most other investors. You will also enjoy the advantage of 'relative certainty.' . . . For most investors, Vanguard will be the place to go." *You've Lost It, Now What? How to beat the bear market and still retire on time*, 2003, p. 62, 70.

Charles D. Ellis, money managers' consultant
"The premise . . . that professional investment managers *can* beat the market  . . . appears to be false. It is a loser's game. ... clients would have done better in a market fund." Returns are "splendidly predictable—on average and over time." *Investment Policy, How to Win the Loser's Game*, 1985, p. 5, 20, 34.

Jane Bryant Quinn, consumer advisor
"I'm a longtime booster of index mutual funds. These funds follow

the market as a whole. Tons of research has shown that most money managers don't beat the markets they invest in, after costs. Maybe your own stocks or funds have excelled in the past couple of years. But in most cases, you've also been taking extra risk. The odds of superior performance are against you, in the long run. Indexing puts the odds on your side." *Los Angeles Business Journal*, May 8, 2000

Charles Schwab founder, discount broker
"I put my money where my mouth is: most of the mutual fund investments I have are in index funds, approximately 75%. My core investments are index funds. Experienced investors have discovered that in any given year, on average, only 20 to 30 percent of mutual funds outperform the market. That is why I recommend index funds…"
Mr. Schwab tells of one of his friends who owned many well-run funds. After keeping track of all the dividends, taxes, reinvestments tax basis and statements, he found he earned the same return as the index of these funds. After selling them all, he bought the index fund. He has "what he wanted in the first place: diversification, tax advantages, one statement, and lower expenses." *Guide to Financial Independence*, 1998, pp. 90, 103, 111.

Motley Fool, Internet site about investing
"Almost **everything** that you will ever read about mutual funds beyond, "Buy an index fund." is superfluous to your long-term success in investing in mutual funds." Fool.com.

Walter Updegrave, senior editor, *Money*
"Mutual fund picking would be easier if there was one you could count on to outperform 70% or so of its competitors over long stretches of a decade or more. It's called an index fund. Although less than 10% of investors own an index fund, they are "one of the best-kept secrets" on Wall Street. My unabashed aim is to convince you to put at least a part of your money into one or more of these funds. You have a far less than a 50% chance of beating the market…. I strongly recommend that you make index funds your primary holding…." *The Right Way to Invest in Mutual Funds*, 1996, p 189-194.

Andrew Tobias, financial writer

"Scrimp and save, putting whatever you can into no-load, low-expense stock market index funds, both U.S. and foreign. You will do better than 80% of your friends and neighbors." *My Vast Fortune*, 1997, p. 158.


## Vanguard and TIAA-CREF

The Masters of Index Funds, The Vanguard Group, is owned by its 18 million shareholders—NOT by a management company—holding over $1.4 trillion assets for institutions and individuals.

Vanguard offers no-load funds with the lowest operating expenses: $9 for each $10,000 compared with $205 per year for some funds. Over 40 years, your $10,000 index fund may grow to $931,000 versus $453,000 for a managed fund. Vanguard.com **800-252-9578** offers *Plain Talk* unbiased guides on many subjects. You can invest automatically from your bank account to your index mutual fund account online. Apply online: STAR minimum $1,000. Your strategy is Simple, Easy and Wise.

TIAA-CREF is the world's largest pension company, primarily for educational and research institutions. With $430 billion in assets, this organization now offers its low-cost products, with the highest service quality, to individuals too. TIAA-CREF holds the highest ratings from the four leading rating agencies. Low expenses and low initial contributions make TIAA-CREF an organization you can stay with for life.

At TIAA-CREF.org, you can make application and begin immediately with an automatic monthly contribution of $100 or more from their bank account. You can follow how the assets grow by themselves from your computer. This makes this strategy Simple, Easy and Wise.


### *Both firms are focused on you, not on manager profits*.

Investing for the long-term (10+ years) creates wealth. But, it requires patience. Successful investors treat investing like a business. They have learned to control their emotions by using an investment policy statement. For financially-independent people, this is an important document.

Your investment policy can be as simple as enabling the

automatic investment option on your application. If you begin by investing $250 a month in the Vanguard 500 Index or the TIAA-CREF Equity Index, you have your investment policy. You will not stop investing in that or other equity funds until you reach your goal. Your will continue the process without touching the money.

## Increase returns and reduce risk

Some clients use the MPT strategy to control risk while increasing returns. Modern Portfolio Theory (Moneychimp.com/articles/risk/riskintro.htm) says that if you put your eggs in different baskets of assets that grow at different times, then the value of all your eggs grows with fewer ups and downs. You can manage the ups and downs of equity funds by buying and re-balancing different ones over time. Higher risk assets are small caps, REITs and foreign stocks. This strategy earns 10-12% with 30% less volatility.

Members assemble asset classes callan.com/research/download/?file=periodic/free/457.pdf that fit their risk-reward tastes. According to this Nobel Prize-winning strategy moneychimp.com/articles/risk/portfolio.htm, a high return asset with a low correlation to other assets in the portfolio can actually reduce the risk of the whole. It may be possible to earn high returns with less risk **overall** as each asset goes up and down. See the example at fool.com/personal-finance/retirement/2007/03/06/5-steps-to-salvage-your-retirement.aspx.

Some clients use this strategy. Dimentional provides the benchmarks for comparisons. Dfaus.com Followers of MPT build a portfolio out of low-cost index funds or ETFs. Researchers found that small and value (high book-value-to-price ratio) stock funds have tended to do better than the market as a whole, but have greater volatility. When combined, volatility may be less.

The past provides only PROBABLE futures. But isn't $2,000,000 (plus or minus $100,000) better than $165,000. Your $250-per-month deposit in the bank for 40 years will be worth about $165,000 after tax compared with about $2 million from investing with no tax. Every child would be better off with $2 million (+/- $100,000) than $165,000 from a bank. Note the 2nd line versus the bottom line:

# Cumulative Wealth

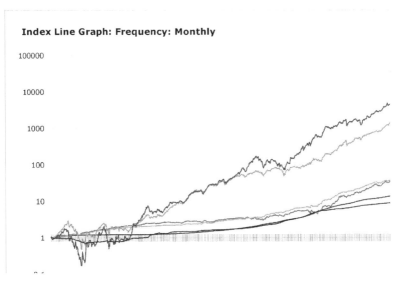

**Index Line Graph: Frequency: Monthly**

Top line—Small Cap Stocks
2nd line—Large Cap Stocks (S&P 500)
3rd line—US Long-term Corporate Bonds
4th line—Intermediate-term Government Bonds
5th line—US 30 day Government T-bills
6th line—US inflation

Courtesy Dr. Campbell R. Harvey http://www.duke.edu/~charvey/

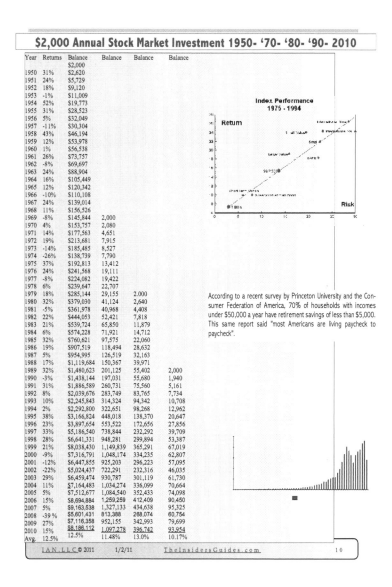

## $2,000 Annual Stock Market Investment 1950- '70- '80- '90- 2010

| Year | Returns | Balance | Balance | Balance | Balance |
|------|---------|---------|---------|---------|---------|
|      |         | $2,000  |         |         |         |
| 1950 | 31%     | $2,620  |         |         |         |
| 1951 | 24%     | $5,729  |         |         |         |
| 1952 | 18%     | $9,120  |         |         |         |
| 1953 | -1%     | $11,009 |         |         |         |
| 1954 | 52%     | $19,773 |         |         |         |
| 1955 | 31%     | $28,523 |         |         |         |
| 1956 | 5%      | $32,049 |         |         |         |
| 1957 | -11%    | $30,304 |         |         |         |
| 1958 | 43%     | $46,194 |         |         |         |
| 1959 | 12%     | $53,978 |         |         |         |
| 1960 | 1%      | $56,538 |         |         |         |
| 1961 | 26%     | $73,757 |         |         |         |
| 1962 | -8%     | $69,697 |         |         |         |
| 1963 | 24%     | $88,904 |         |         |         |
| 1964 | 16%     | $105,449 |        |         |         |
| 1965 | 12%     | $120,342 |        |         |         |
| 1966 | -10%    | $110,108 |        |         |         |
| 1967 | 24%     | $139,014 |        |         |         |
| 1968 | 11%     | $156,526 |        |         |         |
| 1969 | -8%     | $145,844 | 2,000  |         |         |
| 1970 | 4%      | $153,757 | 2,080  |         |         |
| 1971 | 14%     | $177,563 | 4,651  |         |         |
| 1972 | 19%     | $213,681 | 7,915  |         |         |
| 1973 | -14%    | $185,485 | 8,527  |         |         |
| 1974 | -26%    | $138,739 | 7,790  |         |         |
| 1975 | 37%     | $192,813 | 13,412 |         |         |
| 1976 | 24%     | $241,568 | 19,111 |         |         |
| 1977 | -8%     | $224,082 | 19,422 |         |         |
| 1978 | 6%      | $239,647 | 22,707 |         |         |
| 1979 | 18%     | $285,144 | 29,155 | 2,000   |         |
| 1980 | 32%     | $379,030 | 41,124 | 2,640   |         |
| 1981 | -5%     | $361,978 | 40,968 | 4,408   |         |
| 1982 | 22%     | $444,053 | 52,421 | 7,818   |         |
| 1983 | 21%     | $539,724 | 65,850 | 11,879  |         |
| 1984 | 6%      | $574,228 | 71,921 | 14,712  |         |
| 1985 | 32%     | $760,621 | 97,575 | 22,060  |         |
| 1986 | 19%     | $907,519 | 118,494 | 28,632 |         |
| 1987 | 5%      | $954,995 | 126,519 | 32,163 |         |
| 1988 | 17%     | $1,119,684 | 150,367 | 39,971 |       |
| 1989 | 32%     | $1,480,623 | 201,125 | 55,402 | 2,000 |
| 1990 | -3%     | $1,438,144 | 197,031 | 55,680 | 1,940 |
| 1991 | 31%     | $1,886,589 | 260,731 | 75,560 | 5,161 |
| 1992 | 8%      | $2,039,676 | 283,749 | 83,765 | 7,734 |
| 1993 | 10%     | $2,245,843 | 314,324 | 94,342 | 10,708 |
| 1994 | 2%      | $2,292,800 | 322,651 | 98,268 | 12,962 |
| 1995 | 38%     | $3,166,824 | 448,018 | 138,370 | 20,647 |
| 1996 | 23%     | $3,897,654 | 553,522 | 172,656 | 27,856 |
| 1997 | 33%     | $5,186,540 | 738,844 | 232,292 | 39,709 |
| 1998 | 28%     | $6,641,331 | 948,281 | 299,894 | 53,387 |
| 1999 | 21%     | $8,038,430 | 1,149,839 | 365,291 | 67,019 |
| 2000 | -9%     | $7,316,791 | 1,048,174 | 334,235 | 62,807 |
| 2001 | -12%    | $6,447,855 | 925,203 | 296,223 | 57,095 |
| 2002 | -22%    | $5,024,437 | 722,291 | 232,316 | 46,035 |
| 2003 | 29%     | $6,459,474 | 930,787 | 301,119 | 61,730 |
| 2004 | 11%     | $7,164,483 | 1,034,274 | 336,099 | 70,664 |
| 2005 | 5%      | $7,512,677 | 1,084,540 | 352,433 | 74,098 |
| 2006 | 15%     | $8,694,884 | 1,259,259 | 412,409 | 90,450 |
| 2007 | 5%      | $9,163,538 | 1,327,133 | 434,638 | 95,325 |
| 2008 | -39 %   | $5,601,431 | 813,388 | 268,074 | 60,754 |
| 2009 | 27%     | $7,116,358 | 952,155 | 342,993 | 79,699 |
| 2010 | 15%     | $8,186,112 | 1,097,278 | 396,742 | 93,954 |
| Avg. | 12.5%   | 12.5%   | 11.48%  | 13.0%   | 10.17% |

### Index Performance 1975 - 1994

According to a recent survey by Princeton University and the Consumer Federation of America, 70% of households with incomes under $50,000 a year have retirement savings of less than $5,000. This same report said "most Americans are living paycheck to paycheck".

Ibbotson Associates **Stocks average 11.4% per year, bonds 5%, CDs 3%.** Stocks have gone up as much as 54% and as low as –43% in 1 year, up to 28% or down to –12% in 5 years, up 20% or down 0% in 10 years, up 18% or up 3% in 20 years. Short term bonds have gone up 14% or up 0% in 1 year, up 11% or up 0% in 5 years, up 9% or up 0% in 10 years, up 10% or up 1% in 20 years. Large cap stocks have had fewer losing years than treasuries or corporate bonds since 1945.

# Build your **Wealth Reserve**™ with savings from the Insider's Guides:

o Vehicle Insurance . . save up to $6,000 over 10 years
o Homeowner's Insurance . . . $2,000 over 10 years
o Life Insurance . . . $20,000 over 20 years
o Lawsuit Insurance . . . $3,000 over 10 years
o What NOT to buy: 101 products to avoid
o Health Insurance . . . $5,000 over 10 years
o Disability Insurance . . . $5,000 over 10 years
o Long Term Care . . . $40,000 over 20 years
o Education Funding . . . $20,000 over 18 years
o Retirement Spending . . . $1,000s over 30 years
o Banking . . . $3,000 each year
o Annuities . . . $20,000 in 20 years
o Mutual Funds/Securities . . . $3,000 each year
o Spending Plan: Reach every goal
o Self-Funded 'Bank' . . . $250,000 in 15 years
o Vehicle Purchase . . . $10,000 per vehicle
o Mortgage Purchase . . . $3,000 per contract
o **Wealth Reserve**™ . . . $1,000,000 in 25 years
o Wealth Transfer . . . $20,000 in 10 years
o Living Insurance . . . $120,000 over 20 years
o Self-insurance . . . $20,000 over 20 years
o Business Insurance: Buy only what you need
o Financial Independence for Women
o Survivors: Create Your Future Life

www.TheInsidersGuides.com

# 3

## 'Snoring' is the best way to create wealth!

People who are successful have **patience**.

This may seem a simple matter but many people do not realize that you have to be patient in order to cultivate the assets that "grow by themselves." The independently wealthy buy assets that grow; not "things" that require them to pay out income for the rest of their lives. Master investor Warren Buffett said:

We continue to make more money when snoring than when active.
Berkshirehathaway.com

Time rewards you if you are patient. If every parent put just $2,000 in a low-cost stock market index fund at birth, every child might have between $1.2 and $4.7 million by age 65. Parents would not have to do a thing! Depending on the type of fund and account they used, $2,000 could compound at 10% to 12% per year—the historical average. Of course, in 65 years the buying power of $4 million would be about $1 million. Use this calculator to check how investments grows:
moneychimp.com/calculator/compound_interest_calculator.htm
Independents realize that it takes TIME to accumulate wealth. Hollywood exploits our childish fantasy of the instant millionaire. Real "working millionaires" don't get rich overnight. The most common method of making money is use the power of compounding. Independents have memorized the following chart so they know how their dreams will be fulfilled.

## The miracle of compounding

| Monthly | Accumulation at 12% per year | | | | | | | | | |
|---|---|---|---|---|---|---|---|---|---|---|
| | 5 | 10 | 15 | 20 | 25 | 30 | 35 | 40 | 45 | 50 |
| $100 | $8,167 | $23,004 | $49,958 | $98,925 | $187,884 | $349,496 | $643,095 | $1,176,477 | $2,145,469 | $3,905,834 |
| $200 | $16,334 | $46,008 | $99,916 | $197,850 | $375,768 | $698,992 | $1,286,190 | $2,352,954 | $4,290,938 | $7,811,668 |
| $300 | $24,501 | $69,012 | $149,874 | $296,775 | $563,652 | $1,048,488 | $1,929,285 | $3,529,431 | $6,436,408 | $11,717,502 |
| $500 | $40,835 | $115,020 | $249,790 | $494,625 | $939,420 | $1,747,480 | $3,215,475 | $5,882,385 | $10,727,346 | $19,529,169 |

Invest $500 a month in a low-cost stock index fund and accumulate about $1,000,000 in 25 years. Use a tax-favored account like a Roth IRA, and you will pay zero taxes when the money is used. That could mean an extra 25% buying power. What plan could be easier to follow? The only ingredient needed is TIME. This is the essence of **The Simple Financial Life**.

The secret that independents have learned is patience. The vast majority of people with wealth live below their incomes so they can invest some of what they receive. The wealthy spend less than they earn—that's how they stay wealthy. They can't use the miracle of compounding if they spend their money.

## Each $100 invested is worth $10,000 to you in the future

The patient independent person can buy whatever they want because they have planned for the expense. If you wanted to buy a house in 5 years, you could have the down payment of $40,000 by investing $500 a month. If $250 a month is what you can afford now, then it may take 9 years to get that house. Fine, but you could get your house. A bank CD will take you 12 years.

Almost every family wants to own their own home. Independents would be more likely to have the 20% down payment for a new home than others. They save the cost of the PMI insurance required by the lender to cover the lender's risk. Independents are likely to have higher deductibles on all their other insurance so that they benefit from years of saving $500 to $1000 on their premiums by self-insuring part of their risks.

Independents are savvy about saving for major purchases. They are more likely to shop around after doing their homework than to buy because they happen to wander through a store. They are more likely to use balanced and bond mutual funds than a traditional saving account or certificate of deposit. Depending on the amount needed and date of purchase, independents are comfortable using securities to accumulate the cash they need for major purchases. On average, a balanced mutual fund may earn 6-8% per year with more consistency than a stock mutual fund. You can experiment with the amounts and times needed to save for a purchase at moneychimp.com/calculator/compound_interest_calculator.htm. Enter $2000 per year, 30 years, 10 or 12 interest credited 12 times a year and compare what your nest egg could be worth. Enter $6000 ($500 x 12) per year, 10 years, 6% compounded 12 times and compare the result for college or down payment needs.

Finally, independents try to keep their financial lives simple by using only one mutual fund family. Some use only three mutual funds for all their needs. Some use 10. Since you are building this account for long-term accumulation, you should invest in all kinds of companies, around the world. Don't speculate on the hot ones.


## You only need to buy THREE funds

Since independents believe that the cost of investing matters, they buy and hold low-cost stock mutual funds. They make regular and automatic additions to their accumulations. For long-term needs, stock ownership in US and non-US firms provides the best chance of success in accomplishing your goals.

The most efficient way to own companies for long term growth is to buy and hold stock mutual funds that represent the whole world market using "dollar cost averaging" of $100-$500 a month. Over periods greater than 10 years, studies show your returns will exceed those of 86% of investors. An equity index mutual fund with low fees can meet the requirements for long term wealth--$500 a month may reach a million dollars in 25 years if left to compound tax-FREE, using a Roth IRA.

> A **WEALTH RESERVE** may have only three funds

Few mutual fund families offer high quality services to the consistent investor at low cost. The independent investor need look no further than Vanguard or TIAA-CREF for a wide selection of equity funds. They provide exposure to full participation in every sector, and size and style that capitalism has to offer. No one company, sector or poor manager will deplete your accumulation over the long term if you use these firms. Your assets are growing by themselves at the lowest costs.

One fund family lets the new investor start small. Using a Roth IRA account, you can begin with $100 a month at TIAA-CREF. Both fund families earn high marks from financial rating agencies. In fact, Morningstar said, "The firm [TIAA-CREF] is widely known among the institutional crowd, and has a reputation for providing good, low-cost, risk-controlled funds, which this one definitely is. At 0.30%, 'its annual price tag is rivaled only by a scant few competitors', which helps burnish its very investor-friendly profile."

Both firms mentioned above provide long-term performance because less of your money goes to managers, brokers and marketing. The equity funds provide the returns of the market—10% to 12% over any period of over 10 years. There is no guarantee for the future but the probability is very high that stock funds will continue to provide the best hedge against inflation you can buy. Bond funds offer a less volatile return of 6-8% on average. Our strategy takes one hour to execute with either firm. Vanguard offers the Total Stock Market Index, Total International Stock Market Index, and the Total Bond Market Index for simplicity and diversified investing.
**This makes for a Simple, Easy and Wise Plan.**


# Begin TODAY!

Remember the experience of Fred and Susan above. The insurance company executive said that the Reserve they have built up is the real meaning of insurance: it is **lifestyle protection**. He said that today it is even easier to create a **Wealth Reserve**™ because the Roth IRA allows most working people to use market securities for their important needs without paying any federal tax on the earnings—ever. Pension plans delay tax until retirement. You will pay NO tax unless you take the EARNINGS out early.

The **Wealth Reserve**™ Roth IRA lets you pay for a home and disabilities without penalty. You would be able to supplement a smaller Social Security check without any federal income taxes—Zero, Nothing, FREE.

Even if you did not start early, a **Wealth Reserve**™ can be created and used by most people because we are all living longer. The chart on page 39 shows how $166 per month, $2,000 a year has grown since 1950. Even late starters can create a **Wealth Reserve**™ of $249,000 to insure their lifestyle. The table below shows how patience paid off over the years for one client who invested $250 a month in an S&P 500 index account.

## Actual client account, investing $3,000 per year, 1962-2003

| | |
|---|---|
| 24% | 3,720 |
| 16% | 7,795 |
| 12% | 12,091 |
| -10% | 13,582 |
| 24% | 20,561 |
| 11% | 26,153 |
| -8% | 26,821 |
| 4% | 31,013 |
| 14% | 38,775 |
| 19% | 49,713 |
| -14% | 45,333 |
| -26% | 35,766 |
| 37% | 53,110 |
| 24% | 69,576 |
| -8% | 66,770 |
| 6% | 73,956 |
| 18% | 90,809 |
| 32% | 123,827 |
| -5% | 120,486 |
| 22% | 150,653 |
| 21% | 185,920 |
| 6% | 200,255 |
| 32% | 268,297 |
| 19% | 322,843 |
| 5% | 342,135 |
| 17% | 403,808 |
| 32% | 536,987 |
| -3% | 523,787 |
| 31% | 690,091 |
| 8% | 748,538 |
| 10% | 826,692 |
| 2% | 846,286 |
| 38% | 1,172,015 |
| 23% | 1,445,268 |
| 33% | 1,926,197 |
| 28% | 2,469,372 |
| 21% | 2,991,570 |
| -9% | 2,725,059 |
| -12% | 2,403,420 |
| -22% | 1,874,601 |
| 29% | 2,412,905 |

# The Roth IRA Rules

## Contributions:

$5,000 ($6,000 over age 50) each year
Income under $107,000 (2011) single
married $169,000 (2011)

## Distributions:

Tax-FREE for contributions.
And Tax-FREE for earnings if
Over age 591/2,
Account open 5 years,
Taxable earnings unless
Disabled,
First home ($10,000),
Death

## Conversion
IRA, Rollover IRA (401k)
No income limitation
Partial conversion allowed

## Bonus:

Account can grow tax-FREE for life
Minimum distribution rules don't apply
Heirs don't pay income tax
Account has no maximum

Check with your tax preparer
www.IRS.gov/pub/irs-pdf/p590.pdf

# 4

## Self-insure with your **Wealth Reserve**™

There is no better protection than having assets

**This doesn't mean buying a lot of insurance**. It means understanding the role of risk and reward in everyday decision-making. For instance, why pay for medical insurance in your car insurance policy when you already have medical insurance? Independents self-insure the risks they can afford to take.

Self-insurance means retaining part of the premiums and risk of any insurance contract. Many businesses self-insure in order to save money and control the risks of running a business. Many businesses self-insure their group life, unemployment compensation and health insurance. They avoid regulation. They pay a TPA to collect premiums and pay claims from a company account, sometimes in a tax haven. The company earns interest on the money they would have paid as premiums to an insurance company. The business buys a special policy to cover only the huge expenses like heart surgery.

An individual can gain the same advantages by buying high-deductible policies for car, home, health, disability, long-term care, and other insurance. Another form of self-insurance is to reduce the amount of term life insurance over time. This is the concept behind a **Wealth Reserve**™. Instead of paying $375 a month for $500,000 permanent life, a term policy costs $15 a month. You build your $2 million **Wealth Reserve**™ with the $360 balance. When the term becomes expensive by age 50, you can cut the coverage in half and use your own assets to self-insure the rest. By age 65, your kids are grown and your assets provide an income. NO life insurance is needed.

Your **Wealth Reserve**™ will cover your car and home deductibles as well as your supplemental health and long-term care risks. You can actually **drop some of your insurance**. Your **Wealth Reserve**™ protects you against many losses that are small and infrequent. The purpose of insurance is to transfer the risk of catastrophic loss to an entity that pools small premiums from many people to cover one big loss. Many people make the mistake of buying insurance for every single eventuality. Besides complicating your life, this is a waste of money.

Your life insurance policy must insure your life so that your family has an income to survive the transition to a different lifestyle, if you are not around. They need a sufficient amount to generate an income to replace yours. A $500,000 policy could provide $45,000 a year. They may want to pay off all or most of your bills. One term policy costing under $1 a day is sufficient to do this. You don't need insurance on your mortgage, car loan, credit cards, or home improvement loan. See Chapter 8.

Your **Wealth Reserve**™ **replaces permanent life insurance** as your security for the future. Almost every adult can purchase insurance *when* they need it. Contrary to industry hype, cash value life insurance is a terrible investment for a young person. (One viewer of this video said, "I am honestly purchasing whole life insurance from WM  solely due to the music in this commercial." ??!! youtube.com/watch?v=rj6uKxbOy_A&feature=related)


## Create your **Wealth Reserve**™

Save $3,000 a year on financial products you need.
Create a **Wealth Reserve**™ with the savings.
Drop financial products you don't need—you're self-insured.
Self-insure with your **Wealth Reserve**™.

Your **Wealth Reserve**™ consists of all the assets you own that "grow by themselves." A **Wealth Reserve**™ allows you to insure and finance yourself instead of giving your hard won income to your agent, banker or broker. Your **Wealth Reserve**™ allows you to provide for your own permanent life insurance, long-term care insurance, and disability insurance coverage.

Your **Wealth Reserve**™ provides cash for retirement funding. It can even pay for luxury cars, vacation homes and your own business start-up at a discount. Your **Wealth Reserve**™ allows you to buy liability (car and home) insurance at 30% less.

> A **WEALTH RESERVE** provides lifestyle protection

Your **Wealth Reserve**™ allows you to be financially independent like many of our members. It is TIME not investment skill that creates wealth. To repeat Mr Buffett's statement about buy and hold stock mutual funds:

"We continue to make more money when snoring than when active."

berkshirehathaway.com

## How assets build your **Wealth Reserve**™

| Monthly | Accumulation at 12% per year | | | | | | | | | |
|---|---|---|---|---|---|---|---|---|---|---|
| | 5 | 10 | 15 | 20 | 25 | 30 | 35 | 40 | 45 | 50 |
| $100 | $8,167 | $23,004 | $49,958 | $98,925 | $187,884 | $349,496 | $643,095 | $1,176,477 | $2,145,469 | $3,905,834 |
| $200 | $16,334 | $46,008 | $99,916 | $197,850 | $375,768 | $698,992 | $1,286,190 | $2,352,954 | $4,290,938 | $7,811,668 |
| $300 | $24,501 | $69,012 | $149,874 | $296,775 | $563,652 | $1,048,488 | $1,929,285 | $3,529,431 | $6,436,408 | $11,717,502 |
| $500 | $40,835 | $115,020 | $249,790 | $494,625 | $939,420 | $1,747,480 | $3,215,475 | $5,882,385 | $10,727,346 | $19,529,169 |

Financially savvy people buy only the products and services they really need. We show you how they do it in each of the Insider's Guides: banking, mortgage, mutual funds, securities, annuity, life insurance, health insurance, long term care insurance, vehicle insurance, home insurance, lawsuit insurance, vehicle purchases . . . almost any product or service.

You can save up to $3,000 per year using The Insider's Guides. Smart independents don't spend that extra $3,000. They buy "assets that grow by themselves." They put their money into their own business or the stocks of public companies. That $3,000 becomes $3,202, then $6,811, then $10,877, until they have about $100,000 in 15 years. This is your **Wealth Reserve**™.

Financially independent people have fun with their money. They enjoy buying assets that grow without the need to work more hours. They stop wasting their paychecks by making sure that the $3,000 they saved goes automatically into their business or the securities they own. If these independents work for someone else, they continue in their employer's retirement plan when they receive a matching amount for their plan FREE. They start a tax-FREE Roth 401k or Roth IRA.

Where does that extra $250 a month come from? It comes from buying the financial products you really need, directly from quality providers like our insiders do. (theinsidersguides.com/about_us) By buying only what you need directly, without the middleperson, you can identify that $250 a month or more immediately. See the *EasySheet*, below.

One member recently moved their mutual funds from Fidelity to Vanguard and saved over $3,000 a year. They were paying about $4,188 or 1.2% of their account values of $349,000 *each year*. Now they pay less than 0.20% or $698 per year. Their retirement funds will be $545,000 greater because they pay 0.2% instead of 1.2% every year until retirement. Compare your present fund to a low-cost leader to see the difference: https://personal.vanguard.com/us/funds/tools.

## What is a **Wealth Reserve**™?

Your **Wealth Reserve**™ consists of all the assets you own that "grow by themselves." That means your retirement plan at work. It means your rental real estate, your securities and mutual funds. It means your IRAs. It means your business, if you own one. It means your Keogh, SEP, and SIMPLE are your **Wealth Reserve**™ too. Most of your private property--vehicles, appliances, furniture, etc--are **NOT** your **Wealth Reserve**™. They wear out. They don't grow in value. They are expenses from your **Wealth Reserve**™.

Your **Wealth Reserve**™ may consist of many types of assets. In fact financially independent people never put "all their eggs in one basket." Even when they run a business full-time, they typically have only 25% of their wealth in the business. They spread it around —tax-favored retirement plans, rental real estate, and negotiable securities.

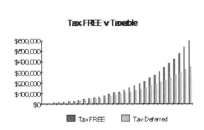

Financially independent people are independent because they use their income to buy more assets that "grow by themselves," NOT more things. Typically their **Wealth Reserve**™ allows them to feel comfortable because they spend less than they make. If their income were to be cut for five or more years, they would be able to survive—keeping their family and home intact. They don't borrow money except to buy assets that earn more than the cost of the loan. Usually a mortgage or business loan is all they owe.

Most of our members use their **Wealth Reserve**™ for the bulk of their retirement plan. Some started early in their working life and consistently increased the proportion of their income designated for investments. By maximizing their 401k retirement plan contributions, they have reduced their taxable income. They pay less income tax now. Some obtain FREE contribution matches from their employer. Their **Wealth Reserve**™ growth is supercharged. However, they pay taxes on retirement money.

Their assets grow because of the extra contributions and because their earnings are not taxed now. The contributions reduce their taxable income each year. Also most of their assets are invested in low-cost mutual funds. They decided which mutual funds to use inside their retirement plans based upon the fact that 86% of fund managers cannot beat the market averages even though they charge over 1.2% extra to try every year. Members favor low-cost index funds. *BusinessWeek* Apr 2009.

Most of our members also own other mutual funds, securities and real estate in various taxable, tax-deferred and tax-FREE accounts. Some have left employers with retirement plans after years of accumulation. Most of them have opened rollover IRA accounts and had the new trustee move the money so they continue compounding without spending it and paying tax. Tax-deferred compounding was all that was available until recently.

Many members now have three or more mutual funds with one company. Some members have seen their **Wealth Reserve**™ grow dramatically over the years even though they don't buy the most publicized funds. Some members invest 10% of their income, some more and some less. Most members with sizable accounts started investing about 5% and increased the percentage as their goals became clear. They saved for their first home down payment, college funds, vacations and cars. Members continue to increase the amount invested by using The Insider's Guides to cut the commissions and fees on their financial service needs.

## How your **Wealth Reserve**™ saves you up to 40%

Financially savvy members have used our Insider's Guide to Vehicle Insurance to help them save up to $6,000 over 10 years. We explain that standard vehicle policies charge for coverage that duplicates existing coverage for most people. We explain what you need and don't need and why to keep the deductible high. We show you where to buy if you have a problem in your record, or you have vehicles "at high risk." If you are a safe experienced driver, you can benefit by switching to certain insurers. One of them has been rated No. 1 in customer satisfaction for 4 consecutive years by JD Power and pays YOU dividends. It has the highest A++ ratings. Why pay extra commission and subsidize other people's poor driving habits?

Not every member can qualify for all 13 categories of savings we list. However, our Insider provides enough "tricks of the trade" to help almost every member save hundreds of dollars. For example, a member in Hewlett,

John K. of New Jersey spent 20 minutes with his new carrier's call center agent. His premium fell **33%** from $2,029.30 to $1,358 for 2 Toyotas with full coverage. The carrier is rated A++ by A.M.Best. Claims service is open 24 hours and it has the same complaint rate as State Farm in New Jersey. A year ago, he saved $567 by switching from another carrier.

NY switched and saved over $1,500 on his three vehicles. Instead of spending that $1,500, he has $125 deducted from his checking account monthly by a low-cost mutual fund trustee. He is using a Roth IRA to shield his earnings from any taxation. His goal is to have an extra $125,000 tax-FREE when he retires to cover his long-term care needs, if any.

This member picked the mutual fund inside his Roth IRA specifically so that his assets grew at a different rate than the other ones he owns in his retirement fund at work. His current **Wealth Reserve**™ is sufficient to "loan" him the money for the $1,000 deductible on his new vehicle insurance policy, should he need it this year. By next year, the $125 a month savings will cover the possible deductible while he earns the capital gains that his insurer used to keep each year. Also his **Wealth Reserve**™ will be growing with an additional $125 per month that he was wasting on the insurance before.

A member from Montclair, NJ used our Insider's Guide to Homeowners Insurance to save $5,000 over 10 years. Again, you probably don't need some of the coverage that is hidden in your existing policy. Our Insider explains what you need and don't need, why to keep the deductible high, and when **NOT to call your agent or insurer**. He shows you where to buy if you have a home "at high risk." If you have never had a claim, you may benefit by switching to a "direct writer." Why subsidize others' claims? In some states, you can save 100% or more by using our Insiders' hints.

Another member in Vermont dropped his life insurance after realizing that his adult children did not need the protection any more. Further, after consulting our Insider's Guide to Retirement Plans he determined to invest aggressively to insure that he would have enough to retire when he wanted to. He used our Insider's Guide to Buying Mutual Funds and Securities to save 1% a year on his choice of mutual funds and brokerage firms.

The $156 a month he was spending on life insurance s now buying assets that **Wealth Reserve**™ "grow by themselves." He is increasing his **Wealth Reserve**™ with money he did not need to spend on insurance. Instead of spending the $156 a month, he is investing it to self-insure his lifestyle. He plans to replace his current car in five years. He read our Insider's Guide to Vehicle Purchases and will save about $10,000 on a luxury sedan. Building your **Wealth Reserve**™ protects you against giving money away to banks, especially the $3,000 to $4,000 in interest most people pay every year on credit cards and car loans.

Making your money work for 10 years in your **Wealth Reserve**™ can provide about $51,000, enough for a home down payment, car, vacation, etc. You will have paid only $30,000 ($3,000 for 10 years) for that $51,000. You borrow from your "bank" to pay cash. See the past market returns on page 39.

## You don't have to have extra money or time

The **Wealth Reserve**™ strategy works because you don't have to *find* new money or 2nd job to build your **Wealth Reserve**™. You use the money you already spend for financial services that you decide you don't need. Instead of buying a car or appliance and paying up to 5 times the price by financing it, you pay cash. However, the cash from your **Wealth Reserve**™ is special. It is 'compounded' cash (the $51,000 described above cost you only $30,000!). You pay less because you planned ahead. See our Insider's Guide to Banking to avoid paying FIVE times the price for financed items.

WARNING: This book offers a strategy to self-insure and self-fund your financial needs. Our Insider's Guides show you how to drop services you may not need. However, before you change your current accounts, make certain that the alternative plan is in place. Do not close the old account/policy until you have tried the services from your new providers and started your <u>Wealth Reserve</u>™.

Typically, members are "buy-and-hold" investors. They do not try to time the market by buying the hot stock or fund. That activity only benefits the brokers and leaves the average investor earning 2.56% according to a <u>DALBARinc.com</u> study. Some members use <u>Modern Portfolio Theory</u> (<u>riskglossary.com</u>) to increase returns as they reduce risk.

Some members have chosen low-cost index funds to keep their **Wealth Reserve**™-building simple. These members believe that broad market indexes provide their best chance of accumulating at 10%-12% annually over the long haul. They don't consider themselves risk takers but are comfortable leaving 100% of their long-term money in stock funds. Their short-term goals are accomplished by funding low-cost balanced funds. They used <u>Morningstar.com</u> to screen for the funds they use.

Other members are very well informed about the compaies in their business field. They keep investing in these few firms over the long-term. They buy stocks with deep discount brokers. Some pay zero commissions. Members explain how they do it in our Insider's Guide to Buying Mutual Funds and Securities.

## How your **Wealth Reserve**™ works

An example of how a **Wealth Reserve**™ works over a lifetime was provided above. Fred and Susan started creating a fund many years before our Network was formed. They started out just saving for their daughter's college expenses at birth. They kept using their 'college fund' for more than just college. They used it like a **Wealth Reserve**™ to self-insure and self-fund their lifetime needs.

This is a summary of the story of how Fred and Susan created and used their **Wealth Reserve**™.

Fred and Susan had a baby—Natalie—in 1975. They lived in lower Manhattan. They wanted to protect their new child's future and to have college money. They picked Dow stocks with the highest yield and the lowest price [<u>dogsofthedow.com</u>]. This was in 1975 or '76.

Dividends were reinvested and the income tax was not outrageous. They invested without a broker in plans called DSP and DRIPS (enrolldirect. now us.computershare.com/). They had $5,000 from gifts and they contributed $6 a day ($350 monthly). Most of the companies they picked allowed them to buy stocks without a broker's fee. By the time Natalie was 18, Fred and Susan had about $300,000.

They kept putting money in each month. During the bad years—you know 1977-78, they had second thoughts. But Susan kept them on track.

They had a car accident a few years after they started and needed money to pay for the policy deductible. They were saving about $200 a year by taking the $1,000 deductible. So they needed to sell $1,000 of stock. They sold stock that was down that year. In fact, I think they did not have to pay any tax on that sale. Anyway, that $1,000 sale did not hurt them. They still ended up with about $300,000. And remember, all this time—18 years—they have saved $200 on their car insurance. That's $3,600 of the $75,600 ($350 X 12 months X 18 years) they invested. That is $300,000 for $75,600 invested.

Like most families, they wanted a house. The cost of the down payment--$15,000—came from Natalie's college fund. They still ended up with about $300,000. But what they found was that some of the stocks had done worse than others. They sold the worst ones, paying little tax on the gain.

They purchased the house with the $15,000 and avoided the mortgage insurance that bankers usually charge those who have less than a 20% down payment. This saved them more money each year too.

In a sense then, part of the $350 they paid each month for the college fund was actually paid for by the savings from the fact they had enough of a down payment not to need private mortgage insurance. They saved on their homeowners by picking a $5,000 deductible and not needing expensive extras, like coverage for jewelry or furs. They saved on credit life, disability, unemployment, and PMI insurance that the mortgage bank tried to add on to their mortgage. All these helped pay for the college fund.

In order to protect the $300,000 fund and all their other assets, Fred found out about umbrella liability insurance. For $210 a year, Susan and Fred would have $1,000,000 coverage in case they were sued and needed to pay a lawyer to defend themselves. Even if the accident was their fault, the policy covered the judgment and the lawyer fees too.

They were finally ready for Natalie to go to college. Of course she didn't need the money all at once. And when she made her decision about where to go to college she chose a very good state college that cost only $10,000 a year.

During this time educational loans were very cheap. So Fred and Susan decided to let the college fund grow—20% to 25% a year—during the 90's. They knew this was unusual because the average gain for Dow stocks was 12% a year. They let the loans grow for the first two years until they could see that they had earned $60,000 for two years straight. We discussed this and decided this can't last. So they sold enough stock to pay the loans and the tax of 20% on the stock earnings. Now they realized they did not have to worry about the college loans any more.

They stopped paying for life insurance policies that she and Fred owned. This saved them another $2,500 a year and they continued to invest the $350 per month. It was getting easier with fewer expenses. As a backup emergency fund, they took out a home equity line of credit that cost them nothing—no fees or closing costs. They pay the market rate only *if* they need to use the line for emergencies.

Susan was disabled within the year. She no longer had disability insurance from work. She was not able to work at all. They decided to cut back on their entertainment, vacation, and hobbies in order to get by on Fred's salary. They also had an emergency expense. They had to sell stock to pay $10,000 for Fred's parent's home repair. The tax on the earnings of the stocks did not push them into the next tax bracket, so they are actually paying much less tax this year anyway.

The next year after Natalie graduated; Susan and Fred decided to start their own business. Fred would work part-time. The college fund—now $600,000 or so—gave them the feeling that they would have incomes until they got the store into the black. The store liability policy was not too bad after Susan picked a higher deductible. Fred's job would provide the health insurance they needed.

The store business allows Fred and Susan to deduct many of the normal expenses associated with their activities. The 'college' fund, no longer for college, allows them to save more on the protection they need for retirement. They attended a seminar on long-term care insurance and decided that they can afford it but don't need it. According to page 6 of the Shopper's Guide they received at the seminar, the chance of Fred needing expensive care is 4%; Susan 13%. [See our Insider's Guide to Long-term Care Insurance.]

If they spent $4,000 a year for up to 30 years, they may never get to use that $120,000 [$2,000 each, times 30 years] because they both are in good health. Anyway, 25% of LTC buyers drop it within two years. So, Fred and Susan put the $4,000 in their tax-advantaged retirement plan, connected with their business. This will add another $600,000 for any emergency, including remodeling their home for easy access and hiring a home health aide. Worst case, they have assets and a business which helps them with health care.


# Lifestyle Protection

A **Wealth Reserve**™ is usually started when people get motivated to save and invest, usually when they have a child. Every one of our members wishes they had started their **Wealth Reserve**™ or 'self-insurance fund' earlier than they did.

The Reserve Fred and Susan have built up is the real meaning of insurance: it is **lifestyle protection**. Today it is even easier to create a **Wealth Reserve**™ because the Roth IRA allows most working people to use market securities for their important needs without paying any federal tax on the earnings—*ever*. The Roth lets you pay for a 1st home and disabilities without any federal income tax or penalty. Contributions are always tax-FREE. Today, members would be able to supplement their pensions with the $900,000 or so they have accumulated without any federal income taxes—Zero, Nothing, FREE.
fairmark.com/rothira/disttop.htm

If you expect to live another 10 years, a **Wealth Reserve**™ can be created and used by most people because we are all living longer. The chart on page 39 shows how $167 per month, $2,000 a year, has grown over a number of years. Even late starters can make a **Wealth Reserve**™ of $249,000 to self-insure their lifestyle in retirement.

If your **Wealth Reserve**™ is not depleted by extra health care costs in retirement and extra living expenses due to a longer life and higher living costs due to inflation, you have the satisfaction of knowing that your Reserve can pass to heirs on a "stepped-up basis." That means NO INCOME tax to heir. The annuity and regular IRA do not afford them this kindness. With an annuity and regular IRA, your heirs will get stuck with the income tax bill on the gains at their tax rate. Your **Wealth Reserve**™ can become the Reserve for their families.

Building your **Wealth Reserve**™ can be done by anyone: Invest as little as $100 a month AND cut out wasteful spending on financial products and services you don't need.

Below is the list of savings that our member, the King family, shared with us. They dropped some of the insurance coverage they didn't need—accident, towing and health on their auto insurance, jewels and furs on home insurance, mortgage insurance called PMI, permanent (whole) life. They raised the deductible for their auto and homeowners insurance. They switched mutual fund companies to save annual fees. They are paying off their credit cards and switching to cards with lower fees. They switched banks and cable/telephone contracts. They are adding $600 a month to their **Wealth Reserve**™. They will have enough for emergencies, accident deductibles and home repairs.

Most importantly, the King family will reach their goals: College funds, Vacation home, Small business startup, Travel, Luxury vehicles, Retirement, Foundation creation, and a Legacy.

Finally, a prudent independent has a legal will to protect their children and a power of attorney to protect themselves when they can't. These documents can be executed by yourself for under $60. nolo.com/index.cfm. The reason you need a will is simply that it makes it easier to gain custody of your child, assets and legacy left by your departed spouse. The reason you need a POA is simply that you need an advocate when you can't make decisions yourself. Usually your spouse will be your advocate. You need a living will for the same reason. The case of Terri Schiavo in 2005 made it clear to all why you don't want Congress deciding what you should have decided yourself.

You must start today. Create your **Wealth Reserve**™ following the steps above. Ruthlessly consider if you really need to pay for each financial product you now pay for. Use The Insiders Guides to decide. They were written by **unbiased advisors** who have nothing to gain from your decisions.

Whether you have some retirement funds already or not, it is in your interest to create and build a tax-FREE **Wealth Reserve**™. If you are still working, it makes sense to take advantage of the Roth IRA or Roth 401k. You can contribute $5,000 ($6,000 over age 50) each year. Growth is not taxed and withdrawals are not taxed. After 15 years, you might have $100,000.

If you are already retired, you can convert a portion of your IRA or rollover IRA to a Roth. Then your funds are tax-FREE in the future. If you are already retired and need supplemental income, you can buy an income annuity immediately and let your **Wealth Reserve**™ grow for 15 years. In this example from the recent past, $100,000 provided $600,000 in 9 years. You could buy another income annuity for $100,000 and keep growing the balance for future needs or emergencies.

## Accumulation 1990-2010 Market Returns

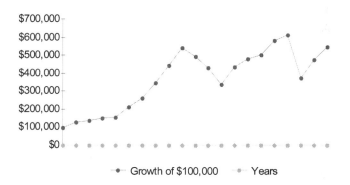

In both situation, you want to keep investing your savings on financial services like mutual funds, insurance and annuities. As a former executive in this industry, I can assure you that our product sellers spent many hours sharpening their skills in separating the mature market from their money. We went after the money. We targeted you to buy variable annuities, insurance and other expensive products with promises of "guaranteed" and "safe" and "never lose money," etc. We studied what you wanted and we tailored the pitch to meet your perceived need.

**EasySheet**  Where your **Wealth Reserve**™ contributions come from:

| Monthly expense savings for the King family: | | | Your family: |
|---|---|---|---|
| Vehicle insurance (2) | $ 56 | | $_____ |
| Homeowners insurance | $ 11 | | $_____ |
| Permanent life insurance | $ 167 | | $_____ |
| Mutual fund fees | $ 83 | | $_____ |
| Mortgage insurance PMI | $ 103 | | $_____ |
| Accident insurance at work | $ 33 | | $_____ |
| Umbrella liability insurance | $ -18 | (bought new) | $_____ |
| Bank fees | $ 10 | | $_____ |
| Credit card finance charges | $ 125 | | $_____ |
| Other fees, charges | $ 30 | | $_____ |
| **Total amount saved monthly** | **$ 600** | | **$_____** |
| **Saved annually** | **$7,200** | | $_____ |

**Possible Wealth Reserve**™ **for the King family**          **Your family:**

**Ten year accumulation**   $139,403          $_____
($7200 for 10 years at 12%)
Goals
        College funds
        Vacation home

**Twenty year accumulation**          $599,489          $_____
($7200 for 20 years at 12%)
Goals
        Small business startup
        Travel
        Luxury vehicles

**Thirty year accumulation**          $2,117,948          $_____
($7200 for 30 years at 12%)
Goals
        Retirement
        Foundation creation
        Legacy

Accumulation estimates assume an investment in a market index fund with the same world economic performance in the future as in the last 50 years. Use this calculator to find how much you can accumulate:
moneychimp.com/calculator/compound_interest_calculator.htm

# 5

## Create your own Self-Funded 'Bank'
### Pay up to 40% less for any item

When you fund your **Wealth Reserve**™, you are creating your Self-Funded 'bank.' It is the assets you have accumulated that "grow by themselves." The assets allow you to finance your lifestyle purchases instead of giving your hard won income to your credit card banker or lender. Your Self-Funded 'bank' allows you to provide cash for college, cars, vacations and your own business start-up–whatever.

Your Self-Funded 'bank' helps you become financially independent. The key to growing assets is TIME, not investment skill or fast trading. Financially savvy people buy only the products and services they really need. They can save thousands of dollars per year by using

> ## Saved 40%
> Ms. Lee wanted to buy a duplex for rental income. She needed $60,000 down payment to avoid PMI. She invested $250 per month for 10 years in her 'bank.' She earned $27,456 on her $30,000 deposit. She bought a two family house for $300,000 and her tenant's rent pays for the mortgage and ½ the utilities. Ms. Lee is so thrilled, she saves $500 in her 'bank' so she can buy a bigger property.

their 'bank' to loan themselves the money for insurance deductibles, cars, a down payment, and any expenses they would normally finance. Smart independents don't waste that extra money on interest and fees. Instead, they use their income to buy assets that "grow by themselves." They put their money in their own business, rental real estate and the stocks of public companies. The savings can become $100,000 in 15 years when invested. If you are smart, you will repay your 'bank' so that you have a Reserve for later expenses. You can use this calculator (moneychimp.com/calculator/compound_interest_calculator.htm) to estimate your accumulations for specific amounts.

Financially independent people *have fun* with their money. They enjoy buying assets that grow without the need to work more hours. They stop wasting their checks by making sure that their money is invested automatically in their 401k, their business, or **Wealth Reserve**™. They enjoy being financially free of money worries so much that they find a way to save another $3,000 a year. Eventually, they don't have to work for someone else—their money does all the work for them.

## Where can you find the $250 a month?

You can learn which financial products you really need and buying them directly from quality providers. By buying only what you need, directly, without the middleperson, you can identify that $250 a month and more.

As I said before, one member of our network moved their mutual funds from Fidelity to Vanguard and saved over $3,000 a year. They were paying about $4,188 or 1.2% of their current account values of $349,000 *each year* for the last 10 years. Now they pay less than 0.20% or $698 per year. Their retirement fund will be $545,000 larger because they pay **0.2% instead of 1.2%** per year until retirement. Broker-sold 'load' funds are **NOT** better. Compare your present funds to a low-cost leader to see the difference: https://personal.vanguard.com/us/funds/tools/costcompare.

## What is a Self-Funded 'bank'?

Your Self-Funded 'bank' consists of the assets you accumulate from your contributions that "grow by themselves." Usually, these are the shares of mutual funds you buy every month. The Self-Funded 'bank' may consist of many types of assets. In fact, financially independent people never put "all their eggs in one basket." They buy different mutual funds holding growth and value stocks, real estate, and other negotiable securities.

Financially independent people are independent because they use their income to buy more assets that "grow by themselves," NOT more 'things.' Typically, their Self-Funded 'bank' allows them to feel comfortable because they spend less than they make. If their income were to be reduced for five or more years, they would be able to survive—keeping their family and home intact. They don't borrow money from traditional banks unless they can earn more than the cost of the loan. Usually a mortgage or business loan is all they use. Never car or personal loans.

## How assets build your Self-Funded 'bank'
### That crazy chart again!

| Monthly | Accumulation at 12% per year | | | | | | | | | |
|---|---|---|---|---|---|---|---|---|---|---|
| | 5 | 10 | 15 | 20 | 25 | 30 | 35 | 40 | 45 | 50 |
| $100 | $8,167 | $23,004 | $49,958 | $98,925 | $187,884 | $349,496 | $643,095 | $1,176,477 | $2,145,469 | $3,905,834 |
| $200 | $16,334 | $46,008 | $99,916 | $197,850 | $375,768 | $698,992 | $1,286,190 | $2,352,954 | $4,290,938 | $7,811,668 |
| $300 | $24,501 | $69,012 | $149,874 | $296,775 | $563,652 | $1,048,488 | $1,929,285 | $3,529,431 | $6,436,408 | $11,717,502 |
| $500 | $40,835 | $115,020 | $249,790 | $494,625 | $939,420 | $1,747,480 | $3,215,475 | $5,882,385 | $10,727,346 | $19,529,169 |

Most of our clients use their Self-Funded 'bank' to supplement their retirement funds, later in life. Typically they started investing later in their working life. They consistently increased the proportion of their income designated for investments because they started late. By starting your fund early, you are maximizing your retirement plan. You are also reducing your taxable income since you use a Roth IRA. You will pay less income tax. If you understand how to invest, you may obtain FREE contribution matches from your employer in a Roth 401k. This will allow you to use your 'bank' to secure your lifestyle without debt.

Your Self-Funded 'bank' may grow tax-DEFERRED (401k) and tax-FREE, so growth is supercharged. Your assets grow because of steady contributions and because the earnings are not taxed NOW. Hopefully, most of your assets are invested in low-cost global stock mutual funds.

Over time, you will see your Self-Funded 'bank' grow dramatically during some years. Even though your mutual funds may not make the headlines, don't sell them and try to buy the ones in the news. Successful investing comes from buying every month so that when the share price is down, you receive more. No one can control the up and down of the markets but you can avoid high commissions and fees on the 'hot' mutual fund of the day. So, avoid buying the hot and then selling when they cool.

## How a Self-Funded 'bank' saves up to 40%

Financially savvy client/members have used our Insider's Guide to

<u>Vehicle Purchase</u> (in our *Guide to Buying Discount Financial Services*) to help them save $20,000 or more on a luxury vehicle purchase. For example, some years ago, Danielle bought a three year old Lexus ES 300 for $16,000 cash. She saved 30% by buying a quality used car. She paid cash.

Note: If she had obtained a 7.5% loan for 5 years, she would have paid $321 per month. Total paid: $19,260 for a $16,000 car. She paid cash from her Self-Funded 'bank.' She used the $321 a month to make money during those 5 years. Danielle,

> **Save 30% or more**
> Danielle of New Jersey spent 40 minutes online to find 3 luxury car candidates within 50 miles of her home. She faxed each seller a bid of $1,000 under the asking price. She got two affirmatives. She found a three-year old Lexus for $16,000. She brought cash within 24 hours of the fax. The dealer's service record was complete.

who set up her 'bank' years ago, earned $26,500 in those 5 years. She did not pay the interest ($3,260) on the loan AND she is ahead by $29,760 less $16,000 or $13,760. This is why the independently wealthy buy luxury used cars for cash from their 'bank.' They keep building the 'bank' with contributions invested by the trustee automatically.

Another member in California dropped his life insurance after realizing that his adult children did not need the protection any more. Further, after consulting our <u>Insider's Guide to Retirement Spending</u> he determined to invest aggressively to insure that he would have enough to retire when he wanted to. He used our <u>Insider's Guide to Buying Mutual Funds and Securities</u> to save 1% a year on his choice of mutual funds and brokerage firms. *The Insiders' Guides to Buying Discount Financial Services: Buy Direct and Save $3,000 Every Year* at theinsidersguides.com/.

The $176 a month he was spending on whole life insurance is now buying assets that "grow by themselves." He is increasing his Self-Funded 'bank' with money he did not need to spend on insurance. Instead of spending the $176 a month on a new car, he is investing it. He plans to replace his current model in five years. He read our <u>Insider's Guide to Vehicle Purchases</u> and will save using the tips of our insider—a real car dealer.

Building your Self-Funded 'bank' protects you against giving money away to banks, especially the $250-$350 in interest most people pay every month on credit cards and car loans. For example, many people will have to pay $161 per month for 10+ years to pay off the average debt of $10,050 at 15%. They will spend at least $19,360 to pay off that $10,050. (If their rate is 25%, they will pay $25,080 for $10,050.) They pay almost **double** for that same $10,050! bankrate.com

But that's not all—THE **REAL COST** IS MORE!

Think of it. If they did not have to use that $161 each month to pay off the $10,050 and $9,310 in interest, they would be able to use the $161 per month to make money. They could have made about *$37,036* in the 10 years using a mutual fund. So the REAL cost of that $10,050 debt is actually $56,396!! The lender gets the $19,360 (to pay the debt over time) and **they gave up** earning $37,036 from the $161 payment per month for 10 years. They gave up the down payment on a house!

**That $10,050 in debt costs most people about $56,396!!!**
                                                             *FIVE TIMES MORE*

Making $250 per month *work* for 10 years in their Self-Funded 'bank' can provide about $51,000, enough for a home down payment, car, vacation, etc. You will have contributed $30,000 ($3,000 for 10 years) for that $51,000. You can borrow from your 'bank' to pay cash for anything. It is special cash. Your **'bank' cash is worth 40% more than you paid for it over time.**

## You don't have to give up a *latte*

If you pay your Self-Funded 'bank' back, you can buy more things you need at "40% off." This strategy works because you don't have to *find* new money to build your Self-Funded 'bank.' You use the money you save from DISCOUNT financial services. Instead of buying a car or appliance on credit and paying up to 5 times the price by financing it, you pay cash. See our Insider's Guide to Banking to avoid paying other bank charges.
Typically, our members are "buy-and-hold" investors. They do not

try to time the market by buying the hot stock or fund. That activity only benefits the brokers and leaves the average investor earning **2.56%** according to a DALBARinc.com study. Some members use Modern Portfolio Theory (riskglossary.com) to increase returns as they reduce risk.

> WARNING: This Guide offers a strategy to self-fund their financial needs. Our Insider's Guides show them how to drop services they may not need. However, before they change their current accounts, make certain that the alternative plan is in place. Do not close the old account until they have tried the services from their new providers.

Some members have chosen low-cost index funds to keep their Self-Funded 'bank'-building simple. These members believe that broad market indexes provide their best chance of accumulating at 12% annually over the long haul. They don't consider themselves risk takers. They are comfortable leaving 100% of their long-term money in stock mutual funds. Their short-term goals are accomplished by funding low-cost balanced or bond funds.

Other members are very well informed about the companies in their businesses or employment. They keep investing in these few firms over the long-term. They buy stocks with deep discount brokers. Some pay $0 commissions. Members explain how they do it in our Insider's Guide to Buying Mutual Funds and Securities. Check how they do it.


## How your Self-Funded 'bank' works

An example of how your Self-Funded 'bank' works over a lifetime was provided in a previous chapter. Fred and Susan started creating a fund many years before they needed it. They started out just saving for their daughter's college expenses at birth. They kept using their college fund for more than just college. They used it to 'self-fund' their lifetime needs. To review how Fred and Susan used their 'college' fund as a Self-Funded 'bank':

1. Fred and Susan had a baby—Natalie—in 1975. They wanted to

protect their new child's future and to have college money.

2. They agreed on buying stocks because they could hold them without paying tax on the increased value until they needed the money.

3. They wanted a house. The cost of the down payment—$15,000—came from Natalie's college fund. They still ended up with about $300,000. They found that most of the $15,000 withdrawal was money they had already paid tax on.

> **THEIR "COLLEGE" FUND BECAME A SELF-FUNDED 'BANK'**

4. They were finally ready for Natalie to go to college. They had $300,000 available for her when she was 18 years old. She made her decision about where to go to college she chose a very good college that cost only $10,000 a year.

5. During this time, educational loans were very cheap. Accordingly, Fred and Susan decided to let the college fund grow —20% to 25% a year—during the 90's. They knew this was unusual because the average gain for Dow stocks was 12% a year. They let the loans grow for the first two years until they could see that they had earned $60,000 for two years straight. They sold enough stock to pay the loans and the tax of 20% on the stock earnings. At this time, they realized they did not have to worry about the college loans any more.

6. As a backup emergency fund, they took out a home equity line of credit that cost them nothing—no fees or closing costs. They pay the market rate only *if* they need to use the line for emergencies.

7. They had to sell stock to pay $10,000 for Fred's parent's home repair. The tax on the earnings of the stocks did not push them into the next tax bracket, so they are actually paying much less tax this year anyway.

8. Susan and Fred decided to start their own business. Fred would work part-time. Susan would work full-time in what she loved— framing people's pictures.

9. The store business allows them to deduct many of the normal expenses associated with their activities. It also allows them to create another pension where they can contribute up to $49,000.

# Lifestyle Protection

A Self-Funded 'bank' is usually started when people get motivated to save and invest, usually when they plan a family or house purchase. Every one of our members wishes they had started their Self-Funded 'bank' earlier than they did. You can make that dream come true for your life by starting your 'bank' now.

Some have started a self-funded 'bank' for their kids. By putting $2,000 in individual stocks or a stock mutual fund for 8 years before age 25, the child could have almost $40,000 by age 30, $100,000 by age 40, $250,000 by age 50, and $1,000,000 by age 65. This does not interfere with the child's or grandchild's own financial aid or retirement savings plan at work. A Roth IRA makes the money tax-FREE.

This self-funded 'bank' provides money for purchasing anything without paying up to 5 times the price in interest and lost earnings. As we have seen, it is easy to create a Self-Funded 'bank' because the Roth IRA allows most working people to use market securities for their important needs without paying any federal tax on the earnings—*ever*. The Roth lets them pay for a 1$^{st}$ home and disabilities without any federal income tax or penalty. Taking their contributions is FREE. If they paid their 'bank' back, they would be able to rebuild the $2,000,000 for tax-FREE retirement income. Also, each year they paid no federal income taxes—Zero, Nothing. fairmark.com/rothira/disttop.htm

A Self-Funded 'bank' can be created even if you did not start early. Late starters can make a Self-Funded 'bank' of $249,790 in about 15 years. Late starters can find the $500 a month contributions just like the King family did—cutting duplicate products and overcharges on their current financial services using our Guides.

If they have repaid their Self-Funded 'bank' in time, it will provide an income in retirement. You can even provide a Self-Funded 'bank' to your heirs tax-FREE as a Roth IRA beneficiary. An annuity or regular IRA do not afford them this kindness. Your heirs will get stuck with the income tax bill on the gains at their tax rate, too.

Start your Self-Funded 'bank' today. Using this strategy, you can be 'bank' President in 30 minutes. Later, when you have determined that your retirement income is adequate, your Self-

Funded 'bank' can become the basis for your own nonprofit § 501I(3) family foundation. http://www.foundationsource.com/

It is the amount we get to *keep* that matters!

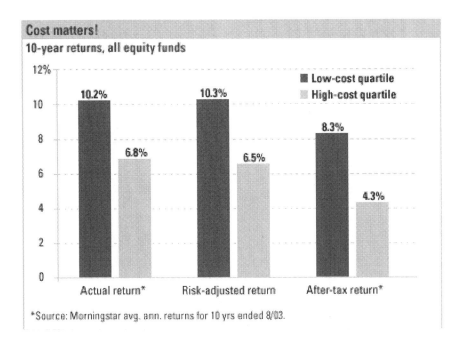

**Cost matters!**

10-year returns, all equity funds

*Source: Morningstar avg. ann. returns for 10 yrs ended 8/03.

# 6

## 12 Things your Agent, Broker, Banker, Advisor and
## Money Manager
### *Will NOT Tell You*

dankeppel.blogspot.com

1. "We have **FEES** and **COSTS** for everything. Most are not necessary." For instance, your life insurance policy is probably one with a higher premium than necessary. Compare the cost of $200,000 benefit for a 50 year old in good health--$356 versus $481 per year. [] It does not cost $50 to buy 200 shares of IBM. You can buy them for $0. [] And why should your broker charge you <u>$160</u> when your account is inactive? [] Why are you paying 50 cents to deposit a check? Banks should pay you to deposit checks. [] Is your <u>401k money manager</u> really worth <u>1.54%</u> of your assets each year? And looses money too? Your employer should buy a retirement plan that costs you $0.30% or less with no <u>kickbacks</u>.

2. "We offer products that are best for *our* firm, not for you. We don't show you all the <u>fees and commissions</u> and financial <u>kickbacks and perks</u> we earn when we sell you our products or you wouldn't buy them. Our products are the "best" available because we sell them. We are the best in the industry because our marketing image says we are." One pension plan provider charges 2.75% a year for their tax-deferred annuity. It has 9 years of surrender charges so you can't transfer your money if you change employers. It charges another $30 a year for 'recordkeeping.' Its mutual funds are among the <u>poorest performers</u>. [] One <u>brokerage</u> firm steered customers into their own funds because they have a higher broker payout. [] Your agent doesn't sell SBLI, your broker doesn't sell Vanguard, your banker does offer really free checking, and your money manager doesn't price your funds at cost—0.1% or less.

3. "We will discuss your financial needs with half truths." You are told you need $1,000,000 of life insurance but the policy type that your agent picks is the most expensive in the world. Even if you

71

agree you need $1 million, you pay more for permanent, 30 year guarantee term or "return of premium" term than just term. [] You want a guaranteed income for the rest of your life but your broker doesn't mention that the annuity payments loose half their value in 24 years. [] You want to save for college but your banker doesn't mention that 529 plans are NOT taxed like the custodial account just opened for your child. You want to save for retirement but your broker put you in two hot funds.

4. "We don't tell you about other alternatives. We don't get paid if we tell you there are less expensive alternative ways to solve your problems." You can buy a FREE checking account from your credit union. The CDs pay more, the checking costs less and the loans are cheaper. You don't need an ATM on every corner. [] You can defer taxation on your account earnings by buying and holding stocks or tax-managed funds. [] You can save on liability insurance by buying only what you need. [] Wealthy people buy "assets that grow by themselves" so they can self-insure and self-fund their needs. [] Consumer Reports reviewed 47 LTC policies and concluded that "for most people, long-term-care insurance is too risky and too expensive."

5. "We don't explain how you can reach your goals in the least costly way." Banks offer life insurance to cover your loan because you want to get the loan. They don't explain that your existing term policy will cover the loan. [] You can build a much larger retirement nest egg by investing in stock mutual funds costing . 07% vs. 1.3%. Compounding magnifies the difference—20% more money over time. [] When new employees sign up for the retirement plan they are encouraged to pick the 'safest' option— treasury bonds. Stocks are more likely to grow in value over the long term than treasuries. Fund rating agency Morningstar found that cost was the best predictor of success.

6. "Our products must be 'sold not bought. We use half-truths in order to contrive an 'urgent financial need' that you can solve only by buying our products." One firm charged a 91-year-old "client" more than $35,000 for four trades over two years, at approximately $8,800 per trade. [] The largest annuity seller is accused of misleading policyholders regarding bonus payments promised on annuity products. [] Life insurance is not the foundation of every

financial plan—you are more likely to run out of money than die in the 21st century. Check broker FINRA

7. "We believe the hype of our own industry: We give good financial advice that you can't get anywhere else." There are no classes in our high schools called Financial Health Class. You can't easily find out the "tricks of the trade" used to sell you the products created to pay high fees to sellers. Young single people don't need life insurance. They need to invest 10% of their income at an early age to reach their goals and become wealthy. [] If brokerage firms actually followed their own stock selection advice, they would have negative returns. The average return for the top 10 brokerage firms was minus 2.26% from 1997-2001! Most were negative (Investars). 86% of managed mutual funds earn less than the market. You are better off making your own mistakes. theinsidersguides.com/

8. "We are experts at figuring out what your "hot buttons" are and using them to get you to buy our products. We exploit the fact that everyone wants to buy the next Google stock or become a millionaire overnight buying and selling real estate or gold. We exploit the fact that seniors fear losing money and want to earn 10% on their money with a completely guaranteed investment." Finding the next Google is

> 'Dumb' money becomes Smart when it learns that low-cost index funds beat the professionals.
> *Warren Buffett*
> (paraphrased)

like finding a dime in a football field on the first try. The average equity investor earned a paltry 2.56% annually; compared to inflation of 3.% and the 9.14% the S & P 500 index earned annually, 1990-2010. [] You pay for guarantees by earning less and not keeping up with inflation. So even though you don't lose money, inflation reduces your money's buying power. Putting your money into different risky investments reduces your chances of losing money and increases your chance of beating inflation. The stock market returns about 11% over time.

9. "We don't sell products from companies that don't pay a commission—so you never obtain the least-cost product. We only sell products with commissions and fees and kickback incentives and "soft dollar" reimbursements." When was the last time your

broker offered the mutual funds with the highest returns over a 20-year period? Vanguard PRIMECAP--13.6% over 20 years--#1 in large company growth stock funds. Vanguard Health--17.4% over 20 years--#1 in Sector funds. Vanguard Energy--16.4% over 20 years--#2 in Sector funds. [] Did your agent call to tell you that life insurance rates are dropping so you should apply? [] Did your auto agent mention that rates have fallen? [] Did your banker mention that internet banking is FREE? [] Where do you find the highest CD rates?

10. "We charge you fees whether we give good service, good rates, good returns, or good benefits." One money manager charges 1.5% for the same exact fund that charges .07%. With $250,000 invested, you will give up about $700,000 (2,723,138 vs. 2,022,979 over 20 years of compounding at market rates). Only 12% of managers can beat their benchmarks over long periods of time. You don't get a refund if your manager can't beat the index. [] You can't get a refund if your CD or annuity renews at a lower rate. [] You can't get a refund if we mess up your trustee to trustee transfer. You don't receive a "better" death benefit check for $200,000 when your loved one dies. [] Many banks hit customers for fees they didn't tell them about. Only the lawyers knew.

11. "When things go wrong, we treat you like you're the enemy." All brokerage firms disallow you to sue for bad service—you must use their arbiter and settle for their decision. One big firm has the worst call response service in the industry. [] One company pressured outside engineers to prepare reports concluding that damage was caused by water rather than by wind. They just denied all of them in the same geographic area. [] Another insurer dropped coverage and stopped signing new policies in coastal areas of 9 states. [] Some long term care insurers aren't paying claims.

12. "We don't care if you have been a loyal customer. We buy and sell customer accounts anytime we can make more money from it." In the last few years, hundreds of customers have had their accounts transferred out of area. For instance, John Hancock's president sold the company to Manulife [Canada], Fireman's Fund was sold to Allianz [Germany], Household Finance went to HSBC [London, Hong Kong], and Sage Life went to Old Mutual [S. Africa]. Brown & Co and HarrisDirect went to E*Trade. Golden

West Financial went to Wachovia to Wells Fargo. MBNA and Fleet Bank went to Bank of America. More consolidation is expected. Your accounts could be next. You can manage your accounts yourself and save:

"Investors should purchase stocks [and financial services] like they purchase groceries—not like they purchase perfume..."
Benjamin Graham, legendary investor

Stocks are the safest investment for periods over 10 years.

Range of annual returns of stocks, 1950 – 2000

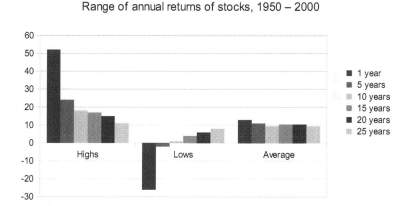

# The Simple, Easy, and Wise Strategy

**Step 1**. Decide how much you can contribute per month or convert each year. It is best to invest each month—NOT all at once. The market could be at its peak on the day you invest a lump sum. Decide which low-fee fund or funds you will buy to start. Equity funds with U.S. and non-U.S. stocks are best for long-term investing.

**Step 2**. Open the Roth IRA account. You could name your spouse as beneficiary and grandchildren as secondary beneficiaries. Later you can change this information. Remember, you must be "employed" to make contributions to a Roth IRA.

Vanguard Roth IRA requires a $1,000 minimum for their STAR index fund. You can open the account online and set up automatic investing from your bank electronically: https://personal.vanguard.com/us/whatweoffer/ira/whichira After your account hits $3,000, you can transfer it to other funds. Call Vanguard Roth IRA 800-551-8631 for help.

TIAA-CREF Roth IRA account can by opened with $100 for the Automatic Investment Plan. Just download the application and send in your first month check. http://www.tiaa-cref.org/ucm/groups/content/@ap_ucm_p_frm/documents/formdoc ument/tiaa01008841.pdf.

Call TIAA-CREF Roth IRA 800-223-1200 for help.
Fidelity Roth IRA account can be opened with $200 for automatic contributions. Just download the application and send in your first month check.
http://personal.fidelity.com/accounts/pdf/brokiraapp.pdf
Call Fidelity Roth IRA 800-343-3548 for help.

**Step 3**. Review your funds annually. Switch contributions to the one that has NOT done well last year—it is a bargain now. Compare your assets level to your plan.

# 7

## The Insider's Guide to Retirement Spending: Assures you of having enough

✓      Insures you have enough assets for the rest of your life, and
✓      Maximizes monthly income for 30 years, and
✓      Accomplishes certain goals for yourself or your family.

## You are more likely to run out of money than die.

A 2002 survey of working and retired pension participants provides reassurance for people who spend time planning for retirement. Those who actually plan tend to have fewer surprises regarding spending needs in retirement than those who don't plan. Tiaa-crefInstitute.org

     The more you have when you begin retirement, the less you have to cut back. Employees with a net worth of more than $1 million expected spending to decline less than 10% at retirement, those with a net worth of $500,000 expected a 15% drop, and those with a net worth of $200,000 expected a 20% drop.

     Actual spending cuts were less than expected. Those expecting to reduce spending about 15% in retirement only experienced a 6% reduction. Those expecting a 20% drop experienced only a 12% to 13% drop. Finally, only 30% of retirees actually experienced a drop. So if your retirement plan relies on having far less expenses, re-think your investment goals in retirement. You may want to continue working and investing for a couple of years to top off all your retirement funds with a **Wealth Reserve**™.

     Market performance has a lot to do with spending levels in retirement. The more of your nest egg that is invested in equities, the more likely your retirement spending will be higher than expected. On the other hand, retirees with no market holdings reported retirement spending in line with expectations. The survey shows that people who plan are less surprised about spending patterns in retirement.

# What we plan for

A retirement spending plan helps those who do not have unlimited wealth live the lifestyle they want to live. A plan means having goals and strategies, including goals to have fun. Accomplishing certain things that you have not had the time or money to do before may be in your plan. One member wanted to start his own business so that he controlled how and when he worked. Another member put aside enough money for medical emergencies and health insurance increases. She had the peace of mind to let her spent all of her pension income. Another started a **Wealth Reserve**™ for each grandchild—gifts so that each had $16,000 in their Roth IRA by age 25. Each will have about $1million tax-FREE. See the compounding growth above.

Other goals that members have written into their plans include establishing an estate plan, providing for a spouse with long-term care insurance, using their **Wealth Reserve**™ to pay for long-term care, establishing a gifting strategy for charities, determining how much of their nest egg to spend each year, and spending a whole month on St. Thomas and Blackbeard's Castle.

Some of these goals required finding and employing a lawyer to make permanent their wishes. However, in most cases, members were guided to do the research and writing of the plans themselves. With this Insider's Guide, we can help you with the process. The financial aspects of your plan are within your mastery. Certain aspects of your plan may require a specialist's advice. Help from some sources is reasonably priced or FREE. vanguard.com/VGApp/hnw/accounttypes/advice or businessweek.com/magazine/content/06_30/b3994406.htm

> A plan assures you will have enough to spend for ever

You have an equal chance of living to 95 as living to age 70 by the time you reach age 65 (7.8 percent vs. 7.7 percent). Women are more likely to live longer. "The fact that the actual length of a retirement period could be 5 years or 30 years dramatically impacts the sustainability of a spending plan," according to the authors of a 2007 study. So, plan for 30 years.

Your plan must include your investing strategy also. Most of us do not have a pension or nest egg of $3 to $5 million so that our lifelong dreams can all come true. About 43% of us may not have enough.

money.cnn.com/2006/06/06/retirement/risk_index/index.htm We have to decide: (1) how much of our principal needs to be invested in the market to offset inflation, (2) how much can safely be withdrawn each month, and (3) should we take Social Security early. bankrate.com/nltrack/news/boomerbucks/20060719a1.asp

Our members have determined the amount to invest in the market to keep pace with inflation and to withdraw monthly. There are investment strategies that provide a reasonable assurance that you can receive an income for life that maintains your lifestyle.

Some members have saved enough for retirement or have a good pension, but don't know how to make sure they have enough to last for the next 30 to 40 years. Our lives are getting longer and that means we have a new problem--**INFLATION**--the price of everything doubles every 20 years.

# Income Sources

Determining your income sources helps you be realistic about your retirement spending plan. Members have discussed the following types of sources of income in retirement: working for others or self, pensions, rollover IRAs, securities, annuities, real estate investments (other than primary residence), personal IRAs (Roth and regular), equity in your home, Social Security, and bank account interest (savings and CDs).

> Keep nurturing your **WEALTH RESERVE**

List your income sources on the **EasySheet** below. This may take a phone call to your employer's human resources area to determine the pension income or lump sum amount. Some employers offer you a choice. You can use this information to compare your best alternative. If your employer went out of business before you start to receive your pension, you might locate it through the pension guarantee fund or pbgc.gov.

Social Security has been sending each of us an estimate of our monthly income annually. If you don't have it now, you used to obtain your statement at ssa.gov. You can also calculate an estimated income online at ssa.gov and ask about your spouse's income at 800.772.1213. When you are ready, you can apply for benefits online too. Remember, you give back $1 for every $2 you earn if you retire early. Financial planners are split on whether it makes sense to work.

If you have left an employer with a pension or 401k or 403b, etc, you had to decide what to do with the money— roll it into your new job's plan or a rollover IRA or keep it there (assuming you didn't spend it). You had to manage the money yourself but you didn't have to pay tax on it. In most cases, you shield it from creditors too.

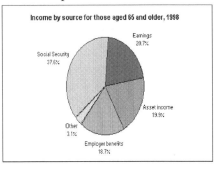

Income by source for those aged 65 and older, 1998

Earnings 20.7%

Social Security 37.6%

Asset income 19.9%

Other 3.1%

Employer benefits 18.7%

## Take Control

Grab all your last statements of the value of your rollover IRAs and securities accounts. Add up the current values so you have a **total nest egg amount** to work with. We call this your **Wealth Reserve**™. It does not have to be exact because we are helping you determine your retirement spending plan. From the estimate, you will know approximately how much income you can expect and if you have a shortfall. You can then decide if you need to invest more, work longer, work part-time, cut your expenses or plan other adjustments. Most members do this by age 62.

If you transferred old pensions or 401k accounts to your new employer, you may be able to borrow from the plan. However, that may cost you dearly since it robs you of the power of compounding the balance of your pension or 401k. [Consider the difference between the amounts in the 35th and 40th year above!] For both kinds of transfer, have the companies do it directly, as a 'trustee to trustee' transfer. Otherwise, the old employer may withhold 20% for taxes you do not need to pay.

If your employer has provided you with a pension income estimate and a lump sum amount, do the next calculation with the lump sum amount added to the total of your IRAs. This will help you decide whether you are better off investing the lump sum with your whole portfolio rather than watching your pension income amount whither with inflation.

The simplest retirement plan would include a pension and social security. If your employer's pension amount is fixed for life, you might need to cut spending later. Even though the social security amount keeps pace with inflation, the pension does not.

If you also have IRAs or annuities, you need to decide how much to withdrawal each year to supplement your income. The accounts may have 50% stock/50% bond funds in order to beat inflation of 3% per year. Many advisors suggest a 4% to 5% annual withdrawal rate as your account grows. This helps your total income keep pace with inflation.

To calculate the estimated income from your nest egg— your principal—and determine if it will last, you need to make certain assumptions. You need to make use of a calculator that runs many tests of your numbers using a probability analysis called:


## "Monte Carlo Simulation"

You can't know the certainty of having enough in the future. You *can* know the probability of maintaining a certain monthly income (adjusted for 3% inflation) for a certain period from a certain lump sum using different proportions of assets.

The assumptions include investment performance, inflation, taxation, your personal needs and objectives. By simulating 500 hypothetical future economic scenarios, the calculator at http://www3.troweprice.com/ric/ric/public/ric.do can help you assess whether your nest egg will last for your life expectancy. (moneycentral.msn.comhttp://gosset.wharton.upenn.edu/mortality/perl/CalcForm.htm) You should discuss your situation with your tax adviser and an estate planning attorney to identify specific issues beyond our general comments. Remember, a plan is a plan, not a guarantee that nothing will change in the next 30 years. Our members are Do-it-yourselfers who make changes.

The larger the percentage of your total income provided by your own investments, the more risk-averse you are likely to be. But remember that you are going to need your principal to grow for 20 or 30 years. In addition, some members want to leave a large estate to their heirs. If this is one of your goals, you should consider using our Insider's Guide to Wealth Transfer. Otherwise, you must increase your nest egg now or lower your withdrawal rate.

On the other hand, if most of your income comes from a pension, you can afford to be more aggressive with your nest egg.

If you have no heirs and no capital-intensive goals, you might wish to plan a financial future based on a higher withdrawal rate. Some members have taken higher rates AFTER their initial lower rates enabled their portfolio to grow beyond expectations. Other members have been guided by the levels of their annual returns. Some have taken more when returns have surpassed 10% for instance. You can change it every year.

The calculator allows you to pick various "portfolio allocations." In the last 50 years, historical averages suggest that using a higher proportion of stocks will increase your income amount. Most of us require payout periods of 20 years or longer. Inflation will cut the amount in half if we don't invest a good part of our nest egg in stocks or stock funds.

Some studies of sustainable withdrawal rates fall into the 7% to 8% level. Most of us would benefit from allocating at least 50% to stock funds. However, inflation-adjusted withdrawals require a lower withdrawal rate from the initial portfolio. Withdrawals of 5% to 6% are more likely to succeed. This assumes that your portfolio has not been significantly reduced at the beginning of your withdrawal period.

Advisors don't have one answer because the future can't be predicted. You have to live with the risks you take; the advisor does not. One member has kept 40% of her assets in stocks, 40% bonds, and 20% short-term investments throughout retirement to assure her family will meet their lifetime income goals. This allocation of assets was tested in over 500 market simulations. Troweprice.com Retirement Income Calculator allows you to test different combinations of assets to see which will produce your monthly income goal. This calculator is useful because the test is done while the calculator increases the income amount to keep pace with inflation over the rest of your life. We discussed suggestions on the composition of your nest egg above.

The calculator also tests all the possible outcomes of your risk-reward asset choices over time to give you a sense of the probability of success. For example, if you have $250,000 at age 65, you can withdraw $1,000 monthly (increasing for inflation) for 25 years with an 80% success rate. In other words, you have a good chance of having enough if you are willing to invest at least half of the funds in stock mutual funds. These assumptions do not include Social Security payments and fixed pension checks. That income stream can maintain a floor to pay everyday expenses like utilities and food. You can increase the probability of success by reducing your initial monthly take.

Fidelity.com also offers a calculator but you must be a member. This version takes you through all income and expense options, including health and long-term care plans. This Guide shortens the exercise for a ballpark assessment. See our Insider's Guide to Long-term Care Insurance to help you decide about insurance.

Ask any retiree about one of his or her major concerns and you are likely to hear about the rise in health care costs. Annual double digit increases are common and increases of 10-15% each year in your health care costs will quickly make a big difference in your ability to live comfortably in retirement. Any plan must address this expense. Cut credit card expenses before retirement.

Another big factor that the inflation rate does not adequately account for is property taxes. Property taxes near Miami went up 46.5% from 2000 to 2004. Will you downsize? (financialsense.com/stormwatch/oldupdates/2004/0716.html) Alternatively taxes in Littleton, Colorado went down 1.6% and residents there pay an average of $1850 instead of the $4549 you could pay in Alexandria.

On the other hand, while you are making sure that you keep expenses and withdrawals low enough to sustain your retirement, you also need to make sure you are withdrawing enough from retirement accounts to satisfy the IRS. Required minimum withdrawals must be taken from your 401(k) and IRA accounts starting at age 70 1/2. Roth IRAs are exempt from this requirement. It makes sense to have your custodian or accountant confirm the required minimum distributions you can calculate at Imagisoft.com or use the IRS.gov rules, pub. 590, page 33. If you don't need the required amount, pop it into a Roth IRA so you don't ever have to pay tax on the earnings again.

Working longer or working part-time can add a cool $100,000 extra to your pot of gold. You are free to quit anytime, especially after a few good years of market returns. Those members who cashed out of the market in 1999 say they are better off now. Do you feel lucky to be able to guess the market level?

## Investment strategy for the rest of your life

What should the level of your market involvement be? Spending in retirement is not really like spending in your pre-retirement years. Don't keep your investments about the same. There should be a change if you are using different assets to lower your overall risk. At age 65, one of you will probably live another 30 years. From an investing point of view, you benefit from inflation-busting stock returns of over 10%. Switching to bonds for safety by retirement age is a traditional strategy. We are living longer. We need growth longer. At least half your portfolio should be in stock funds.

One strategy involves using a set withdrawal rate each year, depending on how well the portfolio does. Thus, you may begin your withdrawals at 5% or 50,000 on a $1,000,000 base. Your second year portfolio has grown to $1,060,000, so you take 5%, which is $53,000. You don't need the money now, so you put the extra $3,000 into a Roth IRA. The year after, the portfolio has decreased to 950,000. You take 5% and live on less. If you have an emergency, you can take money from the Roth IRA tax-**FREE**.

Another strategy relies on a mutual fund company like Fidelity or Vanguard to do the calculations and fund-share selling for you. For instance, with Vanguard's managed-payout funds, investors can expect 3%, 5% or 7% annual distribution. Depending on the fund chosen, you might be satisfied with 5% without eating away of your principal. Fidelity's version would use principal to offer higher amounts of annual income and continue to a certain date in the future. The plan comes with this proviso: "provided the fund's investment strategy works as intended."

The annuity with guaranteed-withdrawal-benefit rider is another strategy. This annuity type, in one case, "guarantees that the buyer can take out up to 8% a year until at least the amount originally invested in the annuity is gone." That works out to about 12 years if the investment doesn't grow. The rider's annual fee of between 0.5 and 0.95 percentage points is steep for the guarantee that you will receive all you paid in. The stock market has produced positive returns for almost every 15-year period since 1950. All these strategies just obscure the calculations with extra fees. They do not guarantee your income or principal will last as long as you need them.

Let's do a reality check on what your future income needs will be. First, you both need to pretend you have retired from your full-time job and list your probable income per month after tax. One of our members provided their data.

They have a home without a mortgage. They will begin

receiving full Social Security benefits at 67 not 65. One spouse has a pension that pays $500 a month. Both have IRAs ($120,000) that might produce $500 a month initially. You can complete the **EasySheet** at chapter end for your numbers.

## This is the monthly income for the Keys:

| | |
|---|---|
| Social Security (2 benefits) | $3,000 |
| Pensions | $ 500 |
| IRAs | $ 500 |
| Other | $ 0 |
| **Total** | **$4,000** |

Could your family live on $4,000 a month or $48,000 a year? This looks pretty good. It assumes that all the big expenses are gone. The house is paid for and the college loans are gone. This assumes that you don't have any medical emergencies and taxes don't go up and Social Security and pensions still pay both of you. Also, this assumes that your IRA withdrawals will meet the required minimum distributions, RMD. Check them annually at kiplinger.com/personalfinance/php/ira/question.htm.

Most people's pensions do not keep pace with inflation. Therefore, you need to make sure that the income you receive will keep pace with inflation. Social Security does keep pace now, but if benefits are reduced in the future to cover increased Medicare costs, you may need to make it up from other sources.

What happens in 20 years? Due to inflation, you will need $8,000 not $4,000 a month to buy the same things. Because of the way you invest your nest egg, it may not be able to keep up with inflation. The $8,000 you need in 20 years may not be there. It would require an extra principal of $120,000 in 20 years to cover the gap that is left because the pension income has no inflation increases or the widow benefit is less.

If someone gave you $120,000 in 20 years, you could withdraw 5% or $6,000 per year or $500 monthly to supplement the pension. This provides you with insurance against higher medical costs and lower Social Security payments. You might need at least $120,000 in 20 years to keep up with inflation and medical cost increases. One of you might need it if the income from a pension and Social Security are reduced due to death.

# Grow $120,000 in 20 years

If you are planning your retirement spending with this Guide **before** retirement, you still have time to insure you have enough. It takes about $125 a month to have $120,000 in 20 years. If you can commit to $125 a month, beginning now, you can relax. That's $8.34 a day. Use the compound interest calculator at moneychimp.com/calculator/compound_interest_calculator.htm to find the amount you need. It shows you how your money can grow. If you begin at age 55, you can have enough by age 75. If you double it, to $250, you may reach $120,000 by age 70. If you live to age 90, you will need to double it again.

Most of our members continue to grow their **Wealth Reserve**™ after they stop working. In a sense, you can't have enough money in the future because you don't know what emergency and health cost increases will come. This is your **'lifestyle' insurance**. The miracle of compounding will provide you with financial independence from now on.

This review of your plan may indicate that you are in great shape financially. Congratulations. If not, fix it today. It takes **TIME**, not a financial wizardry to build wealth. You understand what is needed. We have examples of people who have worked hard to reach a goal that others have considered to be impossible. They play lotto instead of investing just $8.34 a day. Start TODAY.

Members who have enough are those who live below their means, whatever level that may be. Anyone working can become financially independent. We are living longer now. You know you can always use the extra money later on.

Just think of your relatives who are already retired. Do they always have enough? Do they all have a great pension? Do they receive 100% reimbursement on their medical care? Does Medicare cover everything? Are all their prescriptions covered? How about hearing aides? Are medical costs coming down? Have any of your relatives reached 90 years of age? Have any reached 100? Check your life expectancy at http://gosset.wharton.upenn.edu/mortality/perl/CalcForm.html

Even at age 55, if you have done nothing so far, you can each invest $500 a month and in 15 years, you could have $250,000. That can make all the difference later. You will learn to live in financial freedom. It costs only $8.34 a day ($250 monthly). Each dollar is worth $6.25 in your future. It can be **tax-free** too, with a Roth IRA. Make investing automatic so that you are never tempted to stop buying your future independence.

You can be the exception to the vast majority of Americans who will do nothing about this future problem. They will wait for Congress to do something. You are the exception. You understand that in 10 years or more, you will earn more in stock mutual funds than other assets. As you need the funds, move them to your bond or money market fund.

## You are the exception

You are the exception if you know you will be comfortable in your retirement spending. You made a choice. You know how much you need in retirement. You won't have to pay tax on your money in the future with a Roth IRA. You won't fear running out of money in the future. You will be confident because you have planned. Others will have to make cuts in their spending or will need to keep working out of need, **not** out of choice.

| Income annuities may be part of your **WEALTH RESERVE** |
| --- |

One strategy that members have taken is to buy an income or **immediate** annuity that pays you a fixed amount for the rest of your life. Some annuities are designed to increase the amount to keep pace with inflation. However, a less expensive way to make sure inflation does not hurt your buying power is to keep at least part of your nest egg in stock mutual funds. If you use two-thirds of your funds to buy a fixed payment annuity, one-third can keep growing in your portfolio.

One member did this in 2004: She had $300,000 at age 65 to supplement her pension income. She purchased $1,059 per month for life for herself for $200,000. The $100,000 balance may grow back to $300,000 in 10-12 years so she can buy an income annuity again. Annuities are priced at current interest rates so buy when rates are high. Compare annuity income amounts with our Insider's Guide to Annuity Products below.

Medicaid pays for over half of all long-term care expenses. To qualify, you must meet your state's requirements. Generally, those requirements include having an income less than the amount spent by Medicaid for nursing home care. (elderlawanswers.com.) Your spouse gets to keep the primary residence, a vehicle, personal property and some level of assets. In most states, that amount is one-half of the couple's total combined assets, if that one-half does not exceed a certain amount ($109,560 in 2011).

You cannot simply transfer assets to children or others to meet these standards. The state requires that if the gift was made during a period before you apply, Medicaid will not pay until you pay a good part of what you gave away. Exceptions to the transfer rules do exist using a trust or an income annuity. The well spouse can protect their assets and still qualify the ill spouse for Medicaid. A "life estate" can protect your home from estate recovery by Medicaid after both of you are gone. Your kids will still receive the house without capital gains due. See our Insider's Guide to Wealth Transfer below.

You can plan 5 years ahead and make transfers well in advance of needing Medicaid. However, once you give assets away, you can't use them to live on. A careful strategy, developed with an attorney knowledgeable in Medicaid law, will preserve assets while assuring that your spouse receives quality nursing home care. See a local elder lawyer through a referral or their association Naela.com (520-881-4005).

In the 21st century, you are more likely to run out of money than die. Life insurance is not as important as having a nest egg that grows in retirement. Growth is the only way you can be assured of having enough. Members wonder if they can guarantee a lifetime income by buying one "magic bullet." An honest advisor would say THERE IS NO GUARANTEE.

### Saved $120,000

Mr. and Mrs. K., in their 60's, compared LTC with a joint annuity that had a LTC waiver for their needs. The annual cost was $2,000 each for a LTC policy. $50,000 annuity costs 2.5% annually but taxes must be paid by heirs if not used for LTC. Wealth Reserve is tax-friendly now and heirs pay no tax on accumulation of $1/2 million if not used.

However, you can learn to oversee your retirement spending strategy. One member with IRAs and no pension started withdrawing $7,000 a month from his $700,000 nest egg. His nest consisted of 10 different Vanguard funds that had earned over 10%. There is no guarantee but diversification improves your odds. His choices were:

| 2010 Total Return | Fund | Long-term Return | Longevity |
|---|---|---|---|
| 14.9% | 500 Index | 10.6%* | since 1976 |
| 13.4% | Energy | 13.3% | since 1984 |
| 27.4% | Extended Market | 10.6% | since 1987 |
| 6.2% | Health | 16.6% | since 1984 |
| 15.7% | International Growth | 11.4% | since 1981 |
| 12.9% | PRIMECAP | 13.4% | since 1984 |
| 27.7% | Small Cap Index | 10.5% | since 1960 |
| 10.7% | Wellesley Income | 10.2% | since 1970 |
| 14.8% | Windsor | 11.3% | since 1958 |
| 10.6% | Windsor II | 10.5% | since 1985 |
| 15.4% | Average | 11.8% | |

*Average Annual Returns as of 12/31/10.

This member believes that if he can earn at least 11% over time, he will have enough funds to last to age 100. His plan increases his income to $101,000 at age 80 to offset inflation. Request "John's spreadsheet plan" to see his plan: Editor@theinsidersguides.com.

## Summary

1.      Keep 18 months of expenses in a low-cost short-term bond or money market fund (Vanguard.com) with check-writing. personal.vanguard.com/us/FundsSnapshot?FundId=0132&FundIntExt=INT

2.      Pay down all debt. Even if your mortgage provides a tax deduction, you have better uses for your income.

3.      Keep sufficient auto, home, lawsuit, and health insurance to avoid catastrophic expenses. Use our Insider's Guides on each product to save up to $3,000 annually. For instance, members use a Wealth Reserve™ for life, disability and LTC insurance in retirement.

4.      Draw down the required amounts of your tax-deferred plans: pensions, 401K, IRA, SEP, and Social Security. There are penalties for not withdrawing the correct amount.

5.      Sell assets that have lost ground to offset gains first; then long-term taxable, then tax-deferred account assets, finally tax-free. Sell assets to re-balance your overall asset allocation.

6.      If you have sufficient income in retirement, arrange to transfer assets to family members so that they do not have to pay your income or estate taxes upon death.  Use our Insider's Guide to

Wealth Transfer to pass assets without taxes due. Deferred annuities pass to family with income tax owed at the beneficiaries' rates. Our Insider says that 94% of annuity buyers never use their annuity for income. They pass it to family members who are taxed at higher rates.

7.      Establish a small business to do the things you like to do. Your expenses can be deductible from your income and your family gains benefits not available to most retirees. If you need health insurance supplements, educational experiences, travel, transportation, liability insurance, and other lifestyle needs, your business can help provide them.

8.      Create and fund your buy/sell business succession plan to avoid dissolution and unequal legacy assets.

9.      An income annuity will provide a monthly income for life. But you can lose money if interest rates are low when you buy it. It is better to ask your mutual fund family to move a monthly amount into your bank without any annuity fees. You save thousands of dollars in fees and lost interest.

10.     Keep investing in stock mutual funds after retirement. You and your heirs pay no income taxes if you use a Roth IRA.

11.     Confirm that your net assets will not exceed the current federal and state estate tax exemption amount. If they might at your death, you can avoid the tax up to 60% by changing the owner of the assets. A complex estate requires a competent estate attorney. http://www.bankrate.com/brm/itax/news/taxguide/estate-gift-tax1.asp?caret=3g

Use the worksheet provided by the King family to determine if you have enough.

Consider:
You need to make sure that the income you receive will keep pace with inflation. Social Security provides increases to keep pace with inflation. To keep up, the Keys will need $8,000 a month in 20 years. Social Security now says that it may not be able to keep up with inflation after you retire. So, that $3,000 a month will need to be $6,000 in 20 years to buy the same amount as today. You may not receive that much. Also, pensions you may receive may not have COLA (cost of living) increases. The $8,000 you need in 20 years will come up short by $1,500 a month. That would require a principal of $250,000 in 20 years at 12%. A withdrawal of 8% of

$250,000 is $20,000 per year or $1,500 monthly, after tax. This also provides you with "living insurance" against higher medical costs and lower Social Security payments. We think you will need to redirect $250 monthly from spending to investing. Roth IRA earnings are TAX-FREE.

If you smoke, you need to worry about your family having enough. Make sure you have a **Wealth Reserve**™ set up to take care of your family. Term insurance is double the price for you so our Insider (former smoker for 18 years) suggests that you have the **Wealth Reserve**™ ready by age 70. You may require long-term care so make sure your **Wealth Reserve**™ is double the normal amount--usually ten times your highest family income. Smoking costs more than a pack of cigarettes.

# EasySheet
# Will you have enough?

Projected monthly income for the Key family:    Your family:

(Today's dollar value)

| | | |
|---|---|---|
| Social Security (2) | $3,000 | $_____ |
| Pensions (2) | $ 500 | $_____ |
| IRAs | $ 500 | $_____ |
| Securities | $ 0 | $_____ |
| Real estate investments | $ 0 | $_____ |
| Business or job | $ 0 | $_____ |
| Other | $ 0 | $_____ |
| Total | $4,000 | $_____ |

Projected monthly expenses for the Key family:    Your family:

| | | |
|---|---|---|
| Food | $ 300 | $_____ |
| Entertainment | $ 600 | $_____ |
| Travel | $ 400 | $_____ |
| Utilities | $ 200 | $_____ |
| Taxes | $1,000 | $_____ |
| Transportation | $ 200 | $_____ |
| Insurance | $ 400 | $_____ |
| Other | $1,000 | $_____ |
| Total | $4,100 | $_____ |

Extra amount needed per month $ 100      $_____

Extra amount needed per year     $1,200      $_____

Extra amount needed in 20 years $2,400 (inflation 3%)      $_____

Amount invested to produce $2,400 per year:      $_____
$250 per month today

Now you each need to do separate budgets as if you were single. Social Security and most pensions are reduced if the payee has passed away. Some expenses will decrease but many like insurance and utilities stay the same. Make copies of this page and complete them. Women have historically had much lower incomes in retirement because they receive lower fixed payments. "Bag lady" fears are not without foundation. Building a **Wealth Reserve**™ for her is much easier when you have time (compounding) on your side. See our The Insiders Guide for Women and The Insider's Guide for Survivors below.

# 8

## The Insider's Guide to Buying Mutual Funds & Securities:
### Save up to $60,000 over 20 years

✓      Save up to $60,000 in 20 years
✓      Drop "services" you don't need.
✓      Your fund or broker charges fees even when they lose your money
✓      Brokers are salespeople; not unbiased advisors.

### Drop "services" that don't increase your wealth

Our Insider worked for a retail Wall Street firm. He confirms what you knew all along: your broker or mutual fund makes a profit on your relationship whether they help you make money or not. They can't control the market, but you can control their fees and commissions. It is not what you make but what you keep, as the saying goes. There is no proof that a money manager or broker can consistently beat the <u>market,</u> despite the promises. 86% of actively managed mutual funds earn less than the market.
<u>businessweek.com/investing/insights/blog/archives/2009/04/where_have_all.html</u>
The industry charges many commissions and fees (<u>SEC.gov</u>), usually as a percentage of your account total. Fees are taken WHETHER management makes money for you or NOT, whether "<u>service</u>" is good or NOT. <u>jdpower.com/Finance/ratings/full-service-investment-firm-ratings</u> The average total you are paying has risen to 1.52% as the industry has grown. The markets have changed. Your total returns are more likely to be worse when you pay a

> ## Saved $30,000
> Mr and Mrs K of New Jersey transferred all of their mutual fund accounts to the low-cost leader and saved over $3,000 a year in fees. They had been paying 1.2% of their account values each year for 10 years. Their Wealth Reserve will be $545,000 greater because they NOW pay only .20% per year until retirement.

"manager" to manage your money: A 2003 study showed that investors continued to make Wall Street rich by chasing returns and trying to time the market's ups and downs. The study found:

**The average investor earned 2.56%; the market earned 9.14%**

✓  The average equity fund investor earned a paltry **2.56% annually**; compared with 9.14% the S&P 500 index since 1990.
✓  The average fixed income investor earned 1.01% annually; compared to BarclaysAggregate Bond Index return of 6.89%.
✓  It is widely believed that rapid fire trading produces huge profits for traders at the expense of the average investor. But a study shows that market timers actually lose money instead of making healthy profits.
dalbar.com/Portals/dalbar/cache/News/PressReleases/pressrelease040111.pdf

Why do we keep paying more and getting less? Our Insider of 20 years says there are two problems.

1  Paying too much for basic services.
2  Paying for the myth of professional management.

The solution to both problems is available. We can easily learn the secrets of our financial world AND low-cost brokers and funds are now available to all. We can now manage our own investments thanks to discount brokers, ETF and mutual funds. We can even escape taxes with a Roth IRA. Unlike sex education, the basic facts of life—financial **life**— are still not taught to us as teens. Without the

> "Professional money management is a gigantic rip-off."
> Bill Gross, star bond manager
> *Everything You've Heard about Investing is Wrong*

facts, we fall prey to the myths of Wall Street.

You may enjoy the friendship of your broker, banker, or insurance agent. Unfortunately, these salespeople usually don't let us know there are better alternatives to the same type of investments without high fees. Usually this salesperson is not the right person to offer us information on similar products without fees. They depend on the fees for food and shelter. A typical $10,000 transaction provides their firm with revenue of $200 to $5,000 depending on the product. Brokers are expected to bring in at least $100,000 a DAY. They keep less than 30% of the revenue. They are fired if they don't keep selling products for the firm.

Our Insider of 20 years points out that it costs less to run a mutual fund and brokerage firm now than it did 20 years ago. However, the industry *raised* fees and profits. Most mutual fund companies continue to charge 5.75% commission plus 1.5% a year. Many kick back transaction fees and perks to the brokers to keep the business coming their way. aboutbrokerfraud.typepad.com/about_broker_fraud_blog/kickbacks/. As these funds get larger, they become high-cost index funds because they have to invest their $656 billion in the same large businesses that make up the market index. Most funds have returned less than 10% over the last 20 years. Vanguard.com's 500 Index has returned over 10% since 1976 without the commissions. Fidelity's Magellan Fund now lags this index because of its fees. As a whole, the industry returned 9% to investors for the period. You could have saved 2% of your account value or $3,000 on a $150,000 portfolio. See Chapter 2 above.

Our members, Mr. and Mrs. K. of New Jersey, transferred all of their mutual fund accounts to the low-cost leader, Vanguard and saved over $3,000 a year in management fees. They were paying about 1.2% of their current account values of $349,000 each year for the last 15 years. That was $4,188 of the current value. Now they pay less than 0.20% or $698 per year. Their retirement fund will be $545,000 greater because they pay 0.2% instead of 1.2% per year until retirement. Compare your present fund to a low-cost leader to see the difference at Vanguard.com.

It does NOT cost $50 or $30 to for your broker to buy or sell securities and send you a statement, which just obscures what you paid in fees anyway. Few show "annual return" or total costs for trading, management and brokerage staff. However, a few mutual funds and discount brokers have actually reduced costs, some to $0 per trade. They put their clients first. Our members use them and save $3,000 or more a year.

Investing directly through these low-cost firms has become routine for those who are comfortable with their goals and investing strategy. If your investing needs are clear, you can earn the maximum amounts on your money by buying services directly from these firms. You can earn higher returns on your retirement, college funding, savings and investment dollars and you can pay the least for quality products by shopping via the Internet or phone.

# How to earn 10-12%; not 2.56%

We can learn how to become successful investors from the people who are successful. Our members are like the financially independent millionaires in *The Millionaire Next Door*. They do not buy and sell securities. They do not follow salespeople's advice. They make their own decisions. They usually hold securities for many years. They have income from multiple sources: business, securities, rental real estate. nytimes.com/books/first/s/stanley-millionaire.html

Did you notice that the number of millionaires rose to 8 million in 2004, increasing 33% over 2003, a banner year for the market? The primary reason was **NOT** smart stock trading. "Most of the new millionaires had made *few* changes to their portfolios since 2000," according to *Money*, March 2005.

Our Insider says that the people who actually reach their goals let TIME do the work. As Warren Buffett, one of the world's best investors put it, "We continue to make more money when snoring than when active." Berkshirehathaway.com/letters/1996

Actually, you can earn higher returns by NOT picking the top stocks and funds. You are buying high. A buy-and-hold strategy tends to maximize your savings and investing dollars over time. A low-cost fund or discount brokerage account helps you earn more by reducing your costs. It is as simple as that. You can earn 12.22% and **keep 12%** or only 2.56% as the average investor. We suggest you cut out the middle person and skip their advice to buy the "hot" one. You win, they lose.

Of course the industry will dispute that it is just that simple. The industry only makes money when *they* touch your money. The Wall Street myth is that you can't be successful in reaching your goals without their "professional management." The industry highlights the positive star mutual funds and fast-moving stocks, and hides the negative: most managed funds earn 2% less than the market indexes. Most traders lose their money to the industry owners who provide the means of losing, just like casino owners.

Is it really worth learning how the market *really* works and using the buy-and-hold strategy? Can it be that simple? Is it worth the effort and discomfort to switch brokers or mutual funds to save? **You bet it is!** For instance, by using a low-cost mutual fund family like Vanguard, you earn 1-2% more on your nest egg or college fund. Over time, the value of compounding an extra 2% mounts up. Over time, <u>compounding</u> at an average of 12% versus 10% can improve your lifestyle dramatically.

There aren't many funds that can consistently beat the market returns of 10%-12% per year. <u>Vanguard's 500 index fund</u> has done it over the last 15, 20 and 30 years—since its start in 1976. In recent years, it increased 29% and fell 22%. No manager knows what the future will bring but isn't it comforting to know that you can invest in the next best thing to a certainty--the American economy. The 500 index fund holds the largest 500 firms and you can own a share of all of them! Or buy other <u>indexes</u> of the markets (<u>Callan.com</u>). We explained how to do this above.

Thus, smart investors avoid the anxiety-producing hunt for the best fund or stock. **There is none!** Each quarter the best changes. With a <u>low-cost index fund</u>, at least you know you don't overpay. Your funds will **average** 10% per year over

10 years 95% of the time. Can your current fund manager promise that? Low-cost index funds take only $180 per $100,000 account value. Will your current fund manager reduce their $1,500 annual fee when they do a poor job? About 86% of managers produce less than the market averages. Yet we continue to pay them! What a business! ifa.com/12steps/Step3/Step3Page2.asp#333

Actually, Fidelity has decided cost matters so much that it has copied Vanguard's strategy. In 2004, it lowered the fees on some of its index funds to 0.10%. However, before you switch to Fidelity, check the <u>Fidelity.com</u> temporary waiver: "This arrangement may be discontinued at anytime." It is hidden in the second paragraph at the very bottom of the page.

## The money you NOW waste can build wealth!

Our members think they can use the extra earnings rather than Wall

Street. Members who have become financially independent say they wish they had learned how to buy and hold low-cost market-average funds earlier in their lives. Apparently, more people are learning because Vanguard's index funds are among the largest funds in the world, despite the fact that **no** broker, agent or banker sells them!

Members believe that their saving and investing dollars should go DIRECTLY into low-cost mutual funds or index funds traded like stocks (Exchange-Traded Funds or ETF's). Avoid middle persons' fees. Our members share their experiences with indexes in Chapter 2. You find out which securities are recommended by super investors Warren Buffett, Peter Lynch, and Charles Schwab. finance.yahoo.com/etf/education

Successful investor members have their fund manager AUTOMATICALLY debit a monthly amount from their checking accounts. Stock mutual funds help you reach long-term goals like college and retirement funding. Balanced mutual funds can provide cash for all your short-term spending like cars, vacations and emergencies. A balanced (stocks and bonds) mutual fund can compound at 6-8% with fewer ups and downs. personal.vanguard.com/us/funds/snapshot?FundId=0056&FundIntExt=INT

So, investing $250 a month, $3,000 annually for 5 years can compound to $17,500; $50,000 in 10 years. Then you can write a check to buy a vehicle, vacation, or home down payment. To estimate how much you can accumulate, use Moneychimp.com/calculator/compound_interest_calculator. The Insider Guides help you decide to re-direct your current spending on financial services in order to **generate that extra $250 a month to build your Wealth Reserve**™.

Some members use the savings on mutual funds and securities' fees to pay cash for their cars, appliances, vacations, and other goals painlessly. They have built a **Wealth Reserve**™ already. Mr and Mrs K are now celebrating their best years of earnings by cashing in some of their mutual fund shares to buy a vacation home at the Jersey shore.

Our members are using a self-funding strategy for the things they use up, like cars, appliances, and vacations. When you borrow to buy assets that don't grow in value, the cost can be FIVE times the price. The benefit of this strategy is to have your income grow your wealth using compound interest. Building this **Wealth Reserve**™ protects you against giving money away to banks, especially the $3,000 to $4,000 in interest most people pay every year on credit cards and car loans.

Instead, the $3,000 buys assets that "grow by themselves." You avoid giving your hard-earned money to the banker, broker or agent. Making your money work for 10 years in your **Wealth Reserve**™ can provide about $51,000--enough for a home down payment, car, vacation, etc. You will have paid only $30,000 ($3,000 for 10 years) for that $51,000. The difference is the "miracle of compounding." courses.dsu.edu/finance/retire.htm

## You don't have to make a budget or "tighten your belt."

Our strategy works because you don't have to *find* the money to build your **Wealth Reserve**™. You use the money you already spend for financial services that you decide you don't really need. Instead of buying a car or appliance and paying **5 times** the price (financing costs plus the money you did not earn with compounding), you pay "compounded" cash (the $51,000 described above cost you only $30,000!). You pay less because you planned ahead. See our Insider's Guide to Banking to avoid paying 5 times the price.

The savings explained in our Insider's Guides provide the money to grow your **Wealth Reserve**™. Then you can use your Reserve for all major purchases. You turn the amounts that you usually pay the financial services providers into enough money to pay cash for all your needs. You use your income to buy "assets that grow by themselves," not pay fees and interest to make others very wealthy. The recommendations in this Insider's Guide assume that you have or will put your **Wealth Reserve**™ growth on automatic. You can forget it once you start it.

There are many choices in the level of brokerage or mutual fund services you can buy today. You can make your broker rich by picking up the phone and asking what to do with your saving and investing money. Your banker, broker or agent is a salesperson. This nice person is going to offer you the best commission-laden package they have to sell. They won't offer you the best value package because their **firm** doesn't even offer it. Salespeople don't pick the products they sell. The institution picks the products based upon the kickbacks, soft-dollar and other benefits it obtains from the manufacturers. Fidelity brokers were pressured to sell Fidelity

products and some quit: investmentnews.com/apps/pbcs.dll/article?
AID=/20090403/REG/904039959

The last thing a salesperson wants you to do is understand products they don't offer. This is why services are sold as a bundle of services. Very few customers change their initial relationship. The brokerage firm is counting on you NOT shopping for your products/services un-bundled from a low-cost provider. We think you don't need your traditional bank, broker or agent in the 21st century. Think about what that $3,000 a year can do for you—NOT them. You could be giving away **half a million dollars or more in earnings over time.**

The more you buy of what the salesperson recommends, the more you and they feel you have a "great" relationship. Our members have learned not to buy what is offered. They have learned what they need, not what the salesperson has to sell. When our Insider worked with Wall Street brokers, he noticed that most of them couldn't focus on more than 3 products at a time. The firm decides what those three products are. stockbroker-fraud.com/lawyer-attorney-1133786.html The industry mantra is "products are sold not bought." This means there are better alternatives available but they don't pay commissions. Through greed or fear, you are sold them.

## Check your firm and broker with the FINRA.org.

For instance, New Hampshire securities regulators have accused the personal finance advisory unit of American Express of defrauding investors by giving incentives to its advisers to push select mutual funds over other funds with better performance. sos.nh.gov/securities/Press_Releases/PRESSR_2005-02-18.pdf

Our Insider's Guides help you save money by explaining the high-value services you need. The seller wants you to buy the package as presented and leave the details to them. Our members do the opposite: they buy only what they need.

## Advice is the most important benefit

Advice is the most important benefit most people say they pay a broker to provide. However, most don't give good advice. Also, if you have a financial strategy, you don't really need a salesperson in the 21st century. You can have your investing dollars go to your **Wealth Reserve**™ automatically. You can obtain your statement online anytime and at least once a quarter. You guarantee that your spending plan will be accomplished when you invest automatically. Your emotions are removed from the decisions about your long-term strategy.

Your broker and fund manager are not able to predict the future. The analysts they use can't either. *Forbes* 2006 They can't beat the market consistently. They are paid based upon the ***volume*** of money they control, not your returns. The manager makes more as the assets grow. A broker's incentive varies widely among products. There are other perks. The more products and deposits and extras that are handled by your salesperson, the larger the incentives and bonuses they receive. Not even the analysts are paid to be right. They are paid on volume too.

Sales people are trained to handle your objections, not to give you the best alternatives for YOU. They are not in business to provide you with the appropriate service at the least cost. The same services can cost FIVE times as much from one company to the next. Our **EasySheet** below helps you find each service level that is right for you. You can buy low-cost mutual funds and securities by phone or computer in less than 10 minutes DIRECTLY from the manufacturers. Our members have saved $500 in 30 minutes on the Internet. It is safer than sending checks.

This Guide helps you take advantage of our Insider's "tricks of the trade." You probably don't need some services if you evaluate how you use brokerage and fund services. To reach your goals, you need to build your **Wealth Reserve**™. You can build your Reserve by earning more on your account balance by eliminating the extra 1.5% fee you pay now. Your Reserve may be $300,000 to $500,000 larger in 20 years just from that **one small change today**. It is more likely that your market index fund will rise further than your manager's stock picks will rise over time. Plus, you don't have to find the right manager every quarter.

Your **Wealth Reserve**™ is your self-funded 'bank' to buy the things you want. You need to make a plan so that the money will be there when you need it. You can have the money that grew by itself in your **Wealth Reserve**™ because you stopped paying commissions, fees, and interest to your banker, broker, and agent. Start earning cash on your income. You become a creditor not a debtor; a "banker" not a borrower.

Let's talk about the services you really need and where to buy them for less. If you agree that you want to maximize the earning power of your income, then you need to earn money on as much of your monthly income as possible. You need to grow your **Wealth Reserve**™ even when rates and returns are low. You have your choice of investments that provide earnings no matter what the state of the economy. Your employer's 401k may be your one and only investment vehicle. Some employers even give you FREE money to belong. **Take it!**

Do you participate in your employer's retirement (401k, 403b, pension, profit-sharing) plan? Over half of those who are eligible do not. Since many employers match your contributions to some extent, you are throwing money away if you don't accept it. You should consider this money as part of your salary. http://www.401khelpcenter.com/2011_401k_plan_limits.html

Some Network members contribute to their employer's plan even though they don't receive matching funds. They receive TAX-DEFERRAL on contributions up to $16,500 in 2011 (401k) plus $5,000 more if over 50 years of age and they lower their current taxable income. Tax-deferral allows your money to grow faster since there are no taxes to pay NOW. This benefit of qualified plans can mean an extra $570,000 over 30 years (annual investment of $3,000, earning a fixed 10% return compounded monthly).

The flaw in employer tax-deferred plans is the cost structure, which *you* must bear. If your employer has not been careful in selecting a low-cost provider, you can get skinned. The mutual fund company may charge its regular fees plus extra fees to pay for the employer's record keeping and pension consultant. Some mutual funds may be rebating part of the fees you pay back to the plan administrator, according to the SEC.gov in July 2004. Some overpay brokers. The extra costs mean you have 14% to 25% less in retirement. Fees range from 0.35% to 1.72%.

Some members have provided cost comparison information to their HR department at work in order to show how much money is lost. See brightscope.com/ratings/. Our President and Congress people have the best deal. Their index funds (tsp.gov Thrift Savings Plan) charge just 0.05%. Plus, they mandate that those responsible for running the funds be leaders in their fields.

Unfortunately, some plans offer poor investment options and high fees and quarterly or annual charges for all participants. Those with lower salaries pay a disproportionate share of the accounting costs for the plan. The original sales person and the fund management continue to reap huge mark-ups on the assets over 30 or 40 years. Again you may be paying $3,000 a year in fees that rob you of thousands in retirement dollars. One member pays $30 plus 2.49% per year on zero growth since 1999. Her company picked Mass Mutual. If she leaves her job, she must pay 9% surrender charge to transfer money to a rollover IRA.

If you have a choice of investments, consider the cost of the funds you pick. We advocate that you put all your retirement plan money in stock index funds. They are usually the least expensive. Your employer's retirement plan should not be your only investment choice. Avoid buying only company stock. Chapter 2 explains how our members have reached their short-term and long-term goals. There are options that complement your work plan and are TAX-FREE. A **Wealth Reserve**™ with low-cost funds may be a cheaper option because earnings are tax-FREE.


## Buy only the services you need

Your broker, banker, agent or mutual fund firm may ***not*** provide what you need in the 21st century. Our Insider helps you understand financial costs so you can drop what you don't need. In a sentence, you can save enough money in fees and charges on your financial services in order to buy the things you need by letting your money compound FIRST. You turn the tables on the industry. You keep the compound interest on your money instead of your banker, fund manager and insurer.

The financial industry is specializing. Brokers and funds can't earn a profit on your accounts unless you have big balances with them. If you want to become financially independent, decide what you need and buy it directly from the low-cost providers.

If your long-term goals can be met by earning 12% on your long-term money, then you don't need a broker or high-fee mutual funds. If your short-term goals can be accomplished by earning

8%-10%, then you don't need a broker or load funds. You are better off with low-cost mutual funds. You don't need investment fees since no money manager can guarantee high-returns.

If your strategy is to buy and sell individual securities that you think may outperform the 12% average, at least with part of your money, be advised: Brokerage firms do not provide the best research and advice because they make money on trade volume not on stock picking prowess. Brokerage firms develop research to support the **selling** of securities they underwrite for really big fees. Things have not changed since the scandal of 2000-2001, according to analyst Matt Murray. oag.state.ny.us New stock issues (IPO's) are provided to their best institutional customers. Our Insider confirms what Ronald Glantz, former director of research and chief investment officer for PaineWebber (now UBS), told the House.gov back in August 2001.

[Stock] analysts used to view retail customers and investment managers as their clients. Now, the job of analysts is to bring in investment banking clients, **not provide good investment advice**. This began in the mid-1980s. The prostitution of security analysts was completed during the high-tech mania of the last few years.

The financially savvy do NOT listen to the 'experts' because the experts are usually paid to promote certain stocks, not give wise advice. A study by Investars shows how poorly Wall Street firms would do if they *actually followed their own advice*. Nineteen brokerage recommendations were followed from January 1997 to June 2001 while an index of the largest 500 companies gained 75%.


## If Wall Street actually took its own advice!

The average return for the top 10 brokerage firms **was *minus 2.26%*** from 1997-2001! Most were negative. If you owned shares of a low-cost index fund, you would have been ahead 75%. Products are "sold not bought" for a reason!

Savvy asset buyers know that stock analysts and brokerage firms pick stocks they can benefit from praising. As we heard from one of the analysts, Mr. Glantz, above, the analysts promote what their own firms sell. Careers and bonuses are *not* made by being correct forecasters--helping *you* get rich--but by generating revenue for their firms. Things haven't changed as Matt Murray tells in the *NYTimes*, 4/9/6. Bloomberg found S&P 500 companies with the most "buy" ratings gained 8.7 percent in 2010, while the ones with the fewest "buys" jumped 20 percent.

Members who do buy and sell securities use discount brokers AFTER they do their own research. They use discount brokers to make the transactions. They use sites like AAII.com, Morningstar.com, Yahoo.com and Reuters.com to learn about and screen ETF and stocks of companies for possible purchase. Typically they buy and hold quality companies they are familiar with. They have spent hours learning about these firms and the industry. Some hold very few securities. These are just one asset class among many that they own. They like the idea of not "putting all their eggs in one basket."

They use the Internet and their own accountants and lawyers to investigate investments. Like the *Millionaire*[s] *Next Door*, our members do not speculate on stocks or funds. Typically, they do not try to time the market by buying the hot sector or country funds. Some use Modern Portfolio Theory to increase returns as they reduce risk. They illustrate what they do above.

Consider why many savvy investors continue to stuff money into the top 10 no-load mutual funds—most of which are not advertised or promoted: http://www.500indexfund.com/. Are these millions of investors stupid for not listening to their brokers? Compare your total return to these funds.

Some members invest in long-term trends like health-care, age-related recreation, and housing. For instance, one member thinks that the baby-boomer generation will continue to buy RV equipment in order to enjoy travel in North America at their own pace. The member owns the stock of Thor and reads the company reports and information filed with the SEC, as well as industry sites and investor sites like Yahoo and Reuters. Disclaimer: One of our Insiders owned Thor. We are not advocating Thor.

Discount brokers are not created equal. Some have good rates for purchasing a quantity of securities a set dollar amount per month or a set fee to trade anytime or to buy or sell at set times during the day. Depending on your needs, you can buy securities for as little as $0, with some restrictions. You may have an annual fee. Most firms offer automatic monthly purchases and dividend reinvestment. broker-reviews.us/

However, if you only want to buy the stock of one company on a regular basis, you may be able to cut out the brokerage altogether. You can buy directly from the company. Check all the strings attached at Enrolldirect. now us.computershare.com/. Few corporations offer no cost plans.

If you are thinking, "this is a great idea for stocks; what about bonds;" you can buy our government's bonds at TreasuryDirect.gov. You can buy CDs and bonds wholesale at ZionsDirect.com. Recently investors have been offered new corporate bonds paying interest monthly. See Internotes.com.

If "preferred" rates on CDs are your "investments" of choice, you need to shop around. Brokers can make $150 on the CD's they sell you. You can use CD's to maximize your fixed income returns, especially when rates are rising. See our Insider's Guide to Banking to find higher rates.

Brokers now offer mortgages. Mortgage rates are determined by your credit and a buy-down rate (points). You can be overcharged on closing fees. We think you can do better by dealing directly with a mortgage specialist. We help you buy the mortgage you need with our Insider's Guide to Mortgages. If you need money from your home, a home equity line or reverse mortgage may help you.

Borrowing from your broker (margin account) to buy securities is tricky and expensive. If you really believe that your broker can foretell the future and thus borrowing will bring you a windfall, please see the film *Boiler Room* first. imdb.com/

Brokers also offer fee-based accounts. You can trade securities for a fixed fee up to 2.5% depending on the size of your account. Even though your broker has no incentive to churn your account, the firm still rewards the broker for selling certain products. Plus heavy trading doesn't guarantee gains. Most studies show the opposite—your expenses exceed gains.

Another fee-based system called "wrap accounts" claims your money is "managed" by famous managers. However, you will pay dearly for the promise (not fact) of good management. You pay a huge fee, up to 3.5%, whether you make money or not. Usually the minimums are $100,000 so you drop $3,500 or more every year, guaranteed. These managers use models, not your needs, to pick your portfolio, according to our Insider.

The mutual fund wraps are less expensive versions of the promise of higher earnings. Savvy investors don't fall for this one. They go directly to low-cost providers. See members' real asset allocations in Chapter 2.

Many brokerage firms offer single statement cash management accounts, which provide a way to manage all you assets on one platform. Again beware of the fees. Low-cost providers like Vanguard.com and TRowePrice.com also offer this benefit at low cost. You can have your check-writing and ATM card account in one place too. Some discount brokers link your account to an Internet-only bank.

If you rely on a broker to do transactions, keep a copy of all your forms, instructions, confirmations and statements. Take notes of your conversations. We have found that members who ran into mistakes were better off in disputes because they had copious notes. Usually you can only have a hearing with an industry arbitration specialist. You can't sue a broker.

You will notice there are fees for almost everything a broker offers. For instance, if you want a real certificate of a security sent to you, you will pay. It is inconvenient to store and ship certificates yourself.

Monthly fees for a low balance can cost you $1,800 over the years. If you find you have to pay this fee often, it is time to switch account types or brokers.

**This Guide helps you take advantage of our Insider's 'tricks of the trade'.**

Some brokers offer free accounts to start but add fees later. Some deep discount brokers charge fees if you hold small amounts, especially in IRA accounts.

Research and advice from your broker may be your reason for paying higher fees. Now you can receive the information yourself automatically. You can download all the reports that your favorite company has to file with the SEC.gov yourself. You can read press releases and news from Yahoo.com and Reuters.com about your favorite companies automatically BEFORE your broker can send them to you. Brokers rarely have special information just for you. Martha Stewart found out why. Brokers are there to sell you, not advise you.

## Buy only the services you need

1. Mutual funds for long-term accumulation: Vanguard.com and Fidelity.com provide stock and bond funds at the lowest costs.

TIAA-CREF.org and USAA.com offer lower initial investment minimums. Most of these firms offer automatic investing and a full range of products including other mutual funds, individual securities and cash management features such as no-minimum, unlimited check writing and online bill payment. Some offer financial planning and fee-only advisors of top quality at low cost.

2. Brokerage with a purpose. You control your buying strategy with deep discount brokers. Pay the least cost and pick only the services you really need. BuyandHold.com, Scottrade.com, Zecco.com and ING's ShareBuilder.com each have a pricing plan to fit your needs. They may offer a full range of mutual funds and cash management features also. See below.

3. Some brokerage firms charge less if you buy and sell selected ETF and stocks at certain times of the day. Thus BuyandHold charges $2.99 per IRA trades of popular securities only three times a day. Zecco.com offers a wider range of securities in real time for $0—FREE with conditions. See BrokerReviews.us.

4. Full service brokerage firms offer the flush investor all the personal services needed to conduct extravagant lifestyles globally. This includes personal and commercial mortgage, lending, and investment banking. These firms pride themselves on being able to serve countries and their potentates. Financially independent people usually can accomplish their goals without the fees and scandals required by this kind of firm. They will hold hands.

5. Hedge funds are for gamblers. Since the minimums are high and there are only guaranteed costs, consider the odds: 25% fail each YEAR. "Hedge fund investors would have been better off buying an S&P500 Index," according to a recent study. businessinsider.com/hedge-funds-the-emperors-new-clothes-2011-7#ixzz1R40JDlVJ study (economist.com) found that they did worse than the market. Enough said.


## Find the BEST value based upon your needs.

- Internet-only brokers don't have the expenses of branch staff and fancy buildings.

- Mutual funds without private owners can provide lower costs and good service.

Investing in the 21<sup>st</sup> century starts with establishing your own **Wealth Reserve**™. This becomes your lifetime investment portfolio to reach your goals. It can also become your 'bank' for buying things you would normally finance with credit. We are more likely to outlive our money than die, so we are working longer hours. Bls.gov

By investing your income automatically in a portfolio of securities or funds monthly, you can maximize your total wealth without extra money or time or broker. By using low-cost methods like index funds, you can reach your long-term goals like retirement funding and pay for appliances, vacations, and luxury cars when you need them at the lowest cost. Credit cards and loans **ROB** you of your future **compounded asset growth** because you often pay up to **FIVE** times the price of the item. You can accomplish all of your goals by buying "assets that grow by themselves," online directly.

Investing has changed. Brokers are trying to take control of your "asset-management" business, which is extremely profitable. Most brokers or mutual fund managers do not offer the best products in this area. For instance, index mutual funds cost little to run because the manager just holds (not trades) a set list of securities. However, some of the most expensive index funds are sold by banks and insurers.

For instance, one insurance company charged 1.29% per year plus 3% contingency fee for the same performance that Fidelity offers for only 0.10%. That is THIRTEEN times the price for the same thing. You could gain $1.1M for retirement at the low cost provider versus only $0.88M for the same $250 a month over 31 years. Beware of fees. mba.yale.edu/news_events/CMS/Articles/5530.shtml

Each broker, banker and agent dreams of capturing 100% of your financial spending. Your friendly banker, broker, and agent want to sell you every financial product they have to sell even if it is not the best for your financial health. The Internet has made it easier for you to buy the best of what you need. Financially-independent people find better value for their money from firms that specialize. We think that you can find better value by comparing costs and not giving your entire "portfolio" to any salesperson.

The unsung heroes of investing are the mutual fund families that are customer-focused. Only a few firms proved whom they really care about during the 2003 scandal. Vanguard, TIAA-CREF and USAA are operated without a separate owner. Other fund families offer low-cost investments but may be tempted to increase the bottom line by special trading deals. The Attorney General of New York, put it this way:

The full extent of this complicated fraud is not yet known. But one thing is clear: The mutual fund industry operates on a double standard. Certain companies [Bank of America's Nations Funds, Banc One, Janus and Strong] and individuals have been given the opportunity to manipulate the system. They make illegal after-hours trades and improperly exploit market swings in ways that harm ordinary long-term investors. oag.state.ny.us

Governance of the company that owns the funds is THE real issue. At least we know the mission of the three mutual fund firms above.

Vanguard.com Group is owned by its shareholders—NOT a management company, like Fidelity—holding $1 trillion assets for institutions and individuals. Vanguard offers funds with the lowest operating expenses: $20 for each $10,000 compared with $205 per year for the industry.

TIAA-CREF.org is the world's largest pension manager, primarily for educational and research institutions. With $435B in assets, this organization now offers its low-cost products, with the highest service quality, to individuals too. TIAA-CREF holds the highest ratings from the four rating agencies.

USAA.com is a diversified financial services institution owned by its members—armed services personnel and you. Since it is a member-owned organization, without capital stock, serving members is its only concern. It has won many service awards.

Most of our members have found that the least expensive discount broker and the least expensive mutual fund family allow them to maintain total control of their multiple asset portfolios. They enjoy market returns of 10%-12% overall but also like to buy individual issues of companies for which they have special knowledge. These members maintain index funds for broad exposure to the markets and concentrate part of their portfolios in areas that they know well. They know more about some firms than a broker ever will.

Members know that costs are important. You can benefit by shopping for the services you need. The Internet helps you find the broker or fund with the lowest cost for your needs. We think this is better than buying from a broker who calls you. It is easier to know what you want now. The self-funded customer, with a **Wealth Reserve**™ growing larger every month, will find this is the best way to buy the services they need.

The best value for you may be a firm that provides you with special benefits due to your occupation, associations, or situation. For those who qualify, USAA provides brokerage, banking and credit cards. USAA has no agents or offices, yet provides such good service that the industry uses its "best in class" models of processing and service excellence. It was named <u>Best</u> by *Worth* magazine readers.

Many traditional brokers are getting into the act by offering online brokerage services. Most have fees. Most require a substantial relationship to pay for the bricks and mortar too. Direct-to-customer brokers and mutual fund firms are growing and can make it easy for you to interact with them in the way you find convenient. You can invest automatically or by computer in less than 10 minutes. Members think that many of these firms are safer than traditional brokers.

## Shop for low-cost investing services

✓ Save $3,000 per year by using customer-focused mutual funds: <u>Vanguard.com</u>, <u>TIAA-CREF.org</u>, <u>USAA.com</u>. (<u>Fidelity</u> is owned by the Johnson family.)

✓ Shop brokers for every need. <u>BuyandHold.com</u>, <u>TradeKing.com</u>, <u>Scottrade.com</u>, <u>ShareBuilder.com</u>, <u>TDAmeriTrade.com</u>, <u>Etrade.com</u>, <u>Zecco.com</u>, <u>Schwab.com</u> are just the ones our members have used. Beware inactivity fees—e.g. $40.00/quarter, with many exemptions. <u>Discount.broker-reviews.us</u>

✓ Before buying individual bonds, check the prices at <u>Investinginbonds.com</u>, <u>Municipalbonds.com</u>, <u>FINRAbondinfo.com</u>. Research stocks and ETF's at <u>Morningstar.com</u>, <u>FinanceYahoo.com</u>, <u>AAII.com</u>, <u>Reuters.com</u>, or your broker's site. Thrifty members are rewarded by using <u>TreasuryDirect.gov</u>. Check <u>Finance.yahoo.com/etf</u> for ETF's.

✓ Individual securities can also be purchased <u>directly</u> from the companies. See <u>stock1.com/map-bsd.htm</u> or call the companies directly to compare transaction fees. <u>Sec.gov/answers/drip.htm</u>

✓ Earn 8 to 12% mini-lending to people directly. <u>Prosper.com</u> and <u>LendingClub.com</u> are pending. Diversify your income-producing assets.

## Compare at least three institutions for price and service with our EasySheet below.

For bond buyers, full-service brokers may be looking to clean out their inventories and thus already have the bond you want in stock. Firms like Fidelity may charge less commission (even less online), but may have a higher markup to cover the cost of buying the one you want. Edward Jones was rated high by <u>JD Power</u>.

You may be better off with new bond issues only. Some issues have huge markups and some can't be sold easily if you need cash. Some brokers have access to new issues. Some do not. If you are going to trade bonds, you need an experienced broker with inventory at a big firm.

You may find excellent value by buying Treasuries directly and keeping them to maturity. I bonds may be your best buy in a falling interest market. An annuity without a surrender charge can offer another alternative. See our <u>Insider's Guide to Annuity Products</u>. Our Insider can help with your <u>Retirement Spending Plan</u> too.

## Internet brokers are convenient and safe

We recommend you consider using an Internet broker for your securities. Unless you are a professional gambler/trader, you can pay substantially less in fees and commissions over the years. Most members buy and hold stocks so brokers are moving them out of their account books. It just makes sense. Brokers don't make money if you invest wisely: buy and hold.

SAFETY is a key issue. Most have the same SIPC insurance as traditional brokers. PROBLEM resolution is the sticking point as it is with any broker. Try using email to ask questions. How long does it take to get an answer? Members complain more about having to go back to their broker again and again to get the same problem fixed. It takes time to go there and wait for a broker's assistant to fix the problem. Check sites like complaints.com, ConsumerAffairs.com, and epinions.com to see what problems happened in the past. AAII.com members use Scottrade more than others.

## Critical service elements:

1.  Select a broker with SIPC insurance.
2.  Select a broker that will not sell your name and number.
3.  Select a broker that tells you all the costs up front. Big name firms are the worst.
4.  If you're concerned about personal service, some discounters have offices.
5.  Customer "complaints" indicate quality issues.
6.  Confirm you have the best deal for the service you actually use.
7.  Confirm your mutual fund is not a 3-alarm type: http://www.mutualfundobserver.com/

Confirm you have all costs disclosed. See our **EasySheet** below.

# *Caveat Emptor* = Buyer Beware!

## Brokerage disagreements

Using a brokerage firm requires the involvement of many people. Transactions are not complicated but salespeople don't like paperwork. It our experience that every member has had disagreements and problems.
http://www.securitieslaw.com/information/common-complaints.asp
Assume every transaction will get messed up. Most firms accept your money and don't let you sue if there is a problem. investingonline.org Read your account application documents. Our Insider suggests the following:

**1**. Take the time to put your goals and objectives in writing. Most brokers won't ask for them but this statement can protect you later when things go wrong. Send it to the manager too.
**2**. Ask what the small print on all forms means. Disagreements go to arbitration not court. The brokerage firm has the advantage. It is better to ask questions now than try to get your money back later. The industry runs the arbitration process.
**3**. Confirm every order in writing stating what you understand the purpose of the investment is. One member told the broker to sell in 1991 and he did not, even when it was confirmed in writing. Check their record at FINRA.com. The brokerage never made good.
**4**. Ask the purpose and expected outcome of any trade recommended by the broker.
**5**. Check your confirms and statements. Fix any error immediately. **Caveat emptor**. Check dates and amounts for tax reporting. After calling, put it in writing. Copy the manager.
**6**. Take notes of every conversation. Let the broker know you are doing it. You will need documentation when you have a disagreement. Without notes, you will not win arbitration. Brokers are more careful if they know the conversation is being documented.
**7**. Beware commissions and fees. Keep track of them in your log for tax returns Ask the broker for a full breakdown. There are fees for everything except broker calls.
**8**. Insist on a copy of everything. Copy your letters to your broker. Keep literature and anything the broker sends to you.
**9**. Make the portfolio review a must visit. Discuss the progress you are making toward your goals. Discuss the strategy. Ask for

details. Get a written "total return" number annually. Compare it to the appropriate benchmark. You can <u>clear up erroneous information</u> posted to your account. <u>Investingonline.org/aio/complaintcenter</u>

# EasyMove method

This Guide helps you decide which brokerage services you really need. If you have come to the decision that you don't have the best deal, move your account. The best way to do this is gradually.

*First.* Open the new account.
*Second.* Ask for help transferring your portfolio from the old firm. You don't need to talk to your old broker. Some funds cannot be moved since they are proprietary. Re-balance assets with the cash.
*Third.* Contact the old firm's manager by letter. Writing them gives you proof if delays occur.
*Fourth.* Compare your old statement to your portfolio registry. Have all the assets been transferred?
*Fifth.* Ask the new firm to help transfer late dividends and checks from your old account. It may take a month or two. Ask for fee reimbursement.

# NOTES

Date transfer started:

Date completion promised:

Date positions moved:

Date late dividends promised:

Date completion:

# How to Buy Securities For Retirement

1. Cost matters: Broker/advisor cost 1% to 3%

    If you use a salesperson, it can cost HALF A NEST EGG!
    $3,000 per year @11% for 40 years = $2,169,740
    $3,000 per year @10% for 40 years = $1,594,195
    $3,000 per year @9 % for 40 years = $1,179,107

2. Broker/advisor stock picking does not beat index funds over the long run. No money manager has been able to beat the market consistently. No one can forecast the future.

3. Time is the key to investment success. The chance of you buying AND selling, both, at the right times, is near zero.

4. A Tax-FREE investment account increases your balance 25%.

5. Putting all your money in one stock or market sector guarantees failure over time. No investment is perfect.

6. 'Dollar cost average' buying technique lowers the cost of shares over time. When you invest a fixed amount each month, you buy more shares when the price is low and less when high. Over time, you will own more shares at a lower average cost.

# Find out if you have the best value:

|  | Company A | Company B | Company C |
|---|---|---|---|
| Name | | | |

Fees: Annual__ Month__ Per use__
License Check FINRA.org ____ | ____ | ____

Regular account

| | Company A | Company B | Company C |
|---|---|---|---|
|    Market orders | $ | $ | $ |
|    Limit orders | $ | $ | $ |
|    Mutual fund buy/sell fee | $ | $ | $ |
| Options | $ | $ | $ |
| Margin rate | % | % | % |
| Minimum balance required | $ | $ | $ |
| Minimum to open | $ | $ | $ |
| Inactivity fee | $ | $ | $ |
| Tie-in deal or conditions | | | |
|    Bonus | $ | $ | $ |
|    Conditions | | | |
|    Lower loan rate | % | % | % |
| Margin account fee | $ | $ | $ |
| IRA account fee | $ | $ | $ |
| Close ACATS | $ | $ | $ |

Products: Stocks, options, bonds, mutual funds, CDs, muni's, foreign

## Benefits:

| | Company A | Company B | Company C |
|---|---|---|---|
| Credit card with 30-day grace | __ | __ | __ |
| Debit card | __ | __ | __ |
| Bill payment online | __ | __ | __ |
| Bank account link | __ | __ | __ |
| Free fund transfer | __ | __ | __ |
| ATM deposit acceptance | __ | __ | __ |
| Free dividend reinvestment | __ | __ | __ |
| Free check writing money market | __ | __ | __ |
| Free line of credit commitment | __ | __ | __ |
| SIPC protection | __ | __ | __ |
| Complaint process checked | __ | __ | __ |
| Affiliated with other brokerage/bank__ | __ | __ | __ |
| Comprehensive statement | __ | __ | __ |

NOTE: Prioritize the services you use: Buy/sell stocks__ Pay bills__ Hold emergency funds__ Bonds__ Mutual funds__ Research__ Other__ Advice? (See above)

# 10

## The Insider's Guide to Buying an Annuity:
### Alternatives save $20,000 in 20 years

**Buy an annuity ONLY if**

✓ You want a fixed income from a lump-sum **NOW,** or
✓ You have used less expensive ways to save tax-deferred, or
✓ You have a tax-FREE legacy for your family already.
✓ Deferred annuities are taxable to your heirs, at their rates.
✓ Alternative solutions save $20,000 in 20 years.


CAUTION: The U. S. Securities and Exchange Commission took the unprecedented step of publishing a brochure that includes several cautions about buying annuities: "Variable Annuities: What You Should Know," SEC.gov sec.gov/investor/pubs/varannty.htm#vch.

Our Insider of 20 years' experience says many deferred annuity buyers are paying for a guarantee they will never use. The annuity guarantee provides that heirs will receive at least the original investment. However, since almost all annuities are held for over 5 years (the annuity penalty to cancel early is stiff), few buyers experience negative earnings. Most buyers don't get to use the guarantee because they are living longer. If the deferred annuity is left as a legacy, heirs will have to pay income tax at their own rate. This usually negates the effects of the buyer's intent. There are better ways to leave money tax-FREE. We believe you will save over $20,000 with the alternatives in our Insider's Guide to Retirement Spending.

Regardless of how poor deferred annuity earnings may be, the surrender penalties make it likely that you will keep the contract long enough to earn a positive return. In addition to the fees for the guarantee and administration, there are fees for the management of the money and for the seller. The industry's average fee is 2.2% and rising. Most of the "insurance" sold by the industry today is an annuity. It is very profitable. See Stockbroker-fraud.com/morganannuities.htm.

Annuities force you to leave your money with the insurer, which earns the market returns instead of you. Stock and bond market historians found that you would rarely see negative returns for periods over 7 years. Your annuity insurer takes about 2.2% as profit for investing your money in the markets. Inflation takes another 3%. Give yourself a break and keep the fees.

Equity-indexed annuities are really fixed deferred annuities but you don't know in advance what your return will be. The amount you earn will be calculated using a complex formula AFTER a given period. Your money is still invested with the rest of the insurer's portfolio. You pay extra for the guarantee of not losing your original deposit over a 5 to 12 year period, even though there is almost no chance of that happening.

Depending on the surrender charge duration, you may give up some of your principal if you want your money back. The insurer never looses money because *your* earnings are *less* than the insurer's earnings, no matter what the index formula is. The insurer has the use of your money long enough to take advantage of market returns. Over 90% of annuities are never used for income so the insurer keeps taking profits from the use of your money.

**WEALTH RESERVE** can provide tax-FREE income.

The insurer invests most fixed and indexed annuity deposits in stocks and bonds. Over time, insurers earn between 7%-10% annually. Indexed annuity insurers use about 2.5% of the premium to purchase index options. You are credited with interest if the index is high enough during the period you pick. You may earn nothing. Insurers take about 2.5% of the earnings on your deposit as profit and expenses each year. Some annuities pay the seller a commission of up to **17.75%**. Some offer you an incentive to get you started: a first year premium bonus (paid at exit). The agent may also receive incentives like a trip to their favorite resort. Some receive additional commissions each year you keep the annuity. This may give another 1.75% to 3% of your account value to the agent. No wonder annuities sell!

The fixed rate deferred annuity earns interest at a fixed rate set for a certain period of time (1, 3, 5 or 10 years). Insurers set the rate based upon the anticipated return in their portfolio. The buyer of a 1-year annuity is often induced with a bonus, which eventually will be paid for by lower renewal rates. The insurer may adjust your earnings in the final year if you decide to move your money to another insurer. You can transfer to another insurer without taxation by executing a "1035 exchange" from the original insurer.

How do insurers make money? Consider that even before your money is invested, your agent has been paid over $3,000 ($47,000 is the average annuity deposit). The insurer must have a trick to be able to pay out commissions between 4% and 7% of your deposit without earning a dime. The trick is they have your money for a long period of time. Depending on the rules of how your interest is credited to you, the insurer may earn 8% to 10% for over 10 years or an average of $155,000. Most indexed annuities earn 5-7% per year no matter what the agent projects. That means you end up with $77,000 to $95,000 and the insurer keeps $60,000 to $78,000 over that time.

Most financially-independent people would not want to give up almost HALF of the return on their investment for the promise of a base guarantee of only 3%. Few stock or bond index fund have lost money in 10 years so why should you pay $60,000 to $78,000 for a guarantee that you will never use? Our Insider has designed annuities for two insurers. The insurer does not take the risk of losing billions on annuity business if they did not know they could pay the agent, the agency, your premium bonus, the state premium tax, the money manager and the administration costs of the annuity and still make money.

## Better Alternatives

Tax-efficient mutual funds offer "accumulation without taxation" for you AND preserve a favorable tax treatment, called "stepped-up" basis, for your heirs. Lower capital gains taxation upon redemption may prove a gigantic advantage over an extended retirement period. You will not pay the annual 2.2% that the average annuity charges either.

There are no sales charges, surrender and annual charges, including mortality and administrative expenses, policy fees, and the expenses of the variable annuity manager. Vanguard.com and TRowePrice.com offer no-commission tax-managed funds with expenses of 0.15% versus 2% to 3% of your assets each and every year. Your average returns are 10%+ for 5- and 10-year periods versus 4% to 6% for the best annuities.

Another alternative to the deferred annuity is using stock

index mutual funds. Stock index funds are tax-advantaged. Index funds and ETFs cost less than most mutual funds and preserve the **no-income-tax** status for heirs. If you might need the funds for income yourself, you have the benefit of inflation protection. If you need the income, you pay only the 5% or 15% (2010) capital gains tax bankrate.com/brm/itax/tips/20010305a.asp, not the higher income tax rates. **Check new tax rates at IRS.gov.**

Some members have decided to leave a legacy AND keep some funds growing in case they need them later on. They bought a tax-managed fund. Their will dispenses their legacy. See our Insider's Guide to Wealth Transfer. The fact that annuities are being sold by every financial facility around you today does not mean that they are right for you. Annuities are easy to sell and have made their sellers rich. We think this should warn you to look very closely at what you are buying. In fact, some states have banned annuities with high surrender charges and some even want to send the unscrupulous sellers to jail. financial-planning.com/news/floridas-tougher-annuity-fraud-laws-take-2651701-1.html

## What type do you need?

1.  If you may need the funds in 5 years, use the **Fixed** annuity for a set period. If rates are low, pick one year; if high, pick 5 year. Compare CDs bankrate.com/brm/rate/deposits_home.asp.
2.  For longer periods, take a **Variable.** Compare tax-managed funds and tax-FREE **Wealth Reserve**™.
3.  For Immediate income needs, pick an **Immediate Income** annuity.
4.  Use low-cost contracts: no commission, surrender charges, or loads, with low total expenses. Pay 0.25% versus 2.2% annually.

If you can't use the better alternatives in our Insider's Guide to Retirement Spending, the annuity type you need depends on the date you will need the money. Match the annuity earnings to the period of TIME you expect to use the money. If you will need the income in 5 years, a Certificate of Deposit or fixed annuity with low costs is best. If current interest rates are under 6%, use a one-year rate guarantee in anticipation of higher rates. If they are already high, lock in the rate for 5 years.

If you are unsure when you will need the funds, buy a tax-managed fund or low-cost variable annuity. You can split the deposit among stock, bond, real estate and money market accounts. This will protect your earnings over an extended period of time. Beware of the extra management fees for each investment choice in the variable annuity. We believe you will be better off with the index fund choices inside your annuity.

The only **legitimate use of an annuity,** according to our insurance Insider, is the immediate or income annuity. If you need income to supplement your living NOW, buy an immediate income annuity. For instance, a $100,000 deposit might buy $700 monthly payments for life for males, aged 65. This is *dependent* on the interest rates at the TIME of purchase, however. And you cannot "refinance" this contract for a better rate later. If your situation changes, you could use the monthly income to fund a tax-FREE Roth IRA with index funds. Help4srs.org/ may help you break the contract. When rates are low, buy a "10-year certain" contract. Buy another contract when rates improve.

With an income annuity, you could beat the odds and receive 30 years of payments totaling $238,320 for $100,000. However, if you die in 5 years, you forfeit $60,280. A more serious problem is inflation. If you live, your income ($662 a month in this example) will be worth about $330 in 25 years. If you purchase the contract when rates are high (eg: 1983) you would receive about double ($1,141 a month) for life.

Perhaps this is why immediate annuities account for less than 5 percent of all annuities sold. Compare another strategy. Take 7% (initially, $583 per month) from your $100,000 mutual fund account and perhaps leave a legacy. Other options include doing both—at the right time. See our Insider's Guide to Retirement Spending, above, for these and other options.


## How much do you put into an annuity?

If you decide on the annuity, you need to allot as much money into an annuity as your retirement spending plan requires. You can complete your plan in one hour using our Insider's Guide to Retirement Spending, above, to insure you have enough for the rest of your life. The reason you need to make a plan is that none of us knows for how long we will need an income in retirement. Let's say you live to be 90 years old. The income amount you lived on at age 65 will only buy HALF of the same needs at age 90 due to inflation. Your immediate annuity payments will never stop but each payment will buy HALF the goods it did 25 years earlier.

In the same manor, if you receive a pension which is not adjusted for inflation, you will experience a falling standard of living. To offset this slow dollar shriveling, you need to keep growing your assets. Some insurers advertise annuities as an **"income you can't outlive."** The problem is that the fixed amount of the payments will buy less each year. A better solution is to receive an increasing payment stream from a growing asset base like a balanced mutual fund, as we suggested above.

Highlights from our <u>Insider's Guide to Retirement Spending</u>:

1. Keep a fund of cash or the equivalent of 18 months of expenses.
2. Pay down all debt, unless your mortgage provides a tax deduction.
3. Keep sufficient auto, home, lawsuit, and health insurance to avoid catastrophic expenses. Use our <u>TheInsidersGuides.com</u> to save up to $3,000 annually.
4. Draw down the required amounts of your tax-deferred plans: pensions, 401K, IRA, SEP, and Social Security.
5. If you have sufficient income in retirement, arrange to transfer assets to family members so that they do not have to pay your income or estate taxes. Use our <u>Insider's Guide to Wealth Transfer</u> to pass assets without taxes due. Deferred annuities pass to family with income tax owed at the beneficiaries' rates. Our Insider says that 94% of annuity buyers never use their annuity for income. They pass it to family members who are taxed at over 30%.
6. Create and fund your buy/sell business succession plan to avoid dissolution and unequal legacy assets.
7. An income or immediate annuity of about $100,000 will provide about $800 per month for life (10+ years) at age 75. Investing in a money market fund can provide $1,110 a month for 20 years without any annuity fees. You receive more now and leave a tax FREE legacy.

## What to avoid:

✓ Banks, agents, and brokers earn commissions of up to 17.75% of the deposit when you buy their annuities.
✓ Fear of making a "bad" decision with a large lump-sum inheritance or pension rollover.
✓ Not making a comprehensive financial plan for all your assets.

You should avoid any deferred annuity with total fees and charges over 1% a year. You are simply giving money away. If the largest pension provider in the world (TIAA-CREF.org) can provide their annuity for only **0.37%**, you know that the rest of the fees are making someone else rich. Guaranteed "living" benefits add up to 1.10% in annual fees to a variable annuity's typical costs, which range from about 0.7% to 2% of the assets in the annuity. Most benefits can be had without the annuity's high cost.

There are many features used to sell you an annuity. Deferred annuities seem like an attractive way to earn higher returns without risk. However, this is an illusion because the hidden fees sap your money of the power of compounding over time. Studies show you would be better off holding blue chip stocks that pay dividends.

Our Insider has worked for annuity sellers of all kinds. These firms target customers who own bank CDs with the promise of higher rates. Unfortunately, most people actually get to keep less than they are promised. No insurer knows what the markets will bring. Deferred annuity renewal rates often disappoint owners. Sellers know that once snared, buyers will not cancel because of the terrible surrender charges. Sellers exploit most buyers because they are not experienced in investing large sums of money.

The only way to cope with this situation is to have a financial plan that represents your goals and needs for the long **and** short term. If you have a lump-sum coming due, from a job change or settlement or inheritance, your plan will tell you what you need to do with the money. Chapter 2 has a strategy that can be completed in an hour. It shows you what the annuity sellers don't want you to know: there are better alternatives that don't cost you up to half your earnings but provide tax-deferral and/or guaranteed income.

## The Guide to Annuity Guarantees

Variable annuities are increasingly offering a variety of so-called living-benefits guarantees. Here's a guide to the three basic guarantees and what they provide:

| | What it does | Who it's good for |
|---|---|---|
| **Guaranteed Minimum Income Benefits** | Guarantees a minimum level of income, so long as you annuitize the contract at the payout phase. If your account exceeds the guaranteed minimum, you can take a cash payout or annuitize the larger value to create greater income. | For people certain they plan to annuitize their contract and want assurances of a certain level of income in the future. |
| **Guaranteed Minimum Withdrawal Benefits** | Guarantees that you can withdraw a certain percentage of your account every year for a set number of years. Lifetime withdrawal benefits generally guarantee a smaller annual payout, but last until you die. | For people who won't annuitize their contract, but still want guarantees of minimum level of income from their annuity. |
| **Guaranteed Accumulation Benefits** | Guarantees that after a set number of years, typically 10, your account will be worth a minimum level, even if your investments decline. Investment options are generally limited to various asset-allocation models. | For people who want to invest in securities markets, but are concerned about any loss to their principal. |

## Best value:

✓ "Direct insurers" don't have the expenses of their agents and fancy buildings.

✓ Total expenses under 0.5% with no surrender, commission, hidden fee, loads, etc.

✓ Best policy benefits are tax-deferred growth of stock market participation.

✓ Most people don't use the death benefit guarantee or start ('annuitize') the monthly payout from a deferred annuity. Heirs are left paying **your** income taxes at **their** tax rate.

The best value for you if you decide you need a deferred annuity is to buy a low-cost one directly from the top quality firms. If we agree that an income annuity payment in American greenbacks is the same no matter which company pays them, then the decision comes down to a comparison of expenses and fees. If your plan calls for a low-cost deferred annuity, you can download and complete the application in a few minutes.

Our members do a comparison of annuities with the EasySheet below. You want to limit the costs because annuities are a 'cash cow' for insurers. One of our members saved $8,850 over 10 years by buying a deferred annuity from the largest pension company instead of from a nationally-known insurer with a dog mascot. TIAA-CREF has a high financial strength rating. The customer representative who helped our member complete the application (her kids will be the owners, not her, for tax reasons), was licensed and knowledgeable. When she got the contract, she got her questions answered quickly and accurately from the company. She is delighted to save over $9,000 in ten years.

## How and where to buy now

✓ Low-cost annuity firms: TIAA-CREF.org (**800-223-1200**), Vanguard.com (**800-522-5555**), AmeritasDirect.com (**800-555-4655**), Fidelity.com (**800-544-4702**) and Jefferson National (**866-667-0564**) Ukrainian National Association (**800-253-9862**)
✓ Compare monthly income payments at ImmediateAnnuity.com. As of Aug 2011, a 65 year old male receive 7.7% of premium for life guaranteed.
✓ Seek an "underwritten" immediate annuity if health is deteriorated. This type pays a higher amount for life.

Your time horizon should determine which annuity fits your plan. A fixed deferred annuity provides short-term accumulation while a variable offers you the chance to outpace inflation considerably. We believe that low-cost sellers of high quality products offer you the best value. These firms are focused on you. For instance, The Ameritas No-Load Variable Annuity charges less than half of the industry average—just 0.55% and an annual policy fee of just $25. Vanguard provides low cost funds management. Fidelity offers an array of funds inside its variable annuity. TIAA-CREF provides low cost (0.37%) expenses and professional money management as the largest private pension firm. Jefferson National offers a flat fee annuity for life.

Your association and credit union may offer great fixed rate deferred annuities without surrender charges, maintenance or administrative fees. These not-for-profits have membership requirements, which may be worth the cost and inconvenience. For instance, Ukrainian National Association (**800-253-9862**) provides multi-year annuities with rates that beat most CDs.

Many nationally-known insurers offer variable annuities with the option to use the same Fidelity and Vanguard funds inside the contract. However, they usually add another layer of fees with no additional benefits to you. This is one of the reasons that buying an annuity from your insurance agent or banker or broker is **only going to enrich them**. If the actual cost of doing business is about 0.37% of your deposit, you know where the balance of the 2.2% fees is going! You will be paying for the sellers 'advice' for the rest of your life.

## The critical policy elements:

1. Select a company with a high financial strength rating. Use "A" firms.
2. Variable annuities with a fixed return option allow the "best of both worlds."
3. Choose extras carefully. The annual fees rob you of the benefits (tax-deferred compounding) you are paying extra for.
4. Know the salesperson. Contact Finra.org/Investors/index.htm 800-289-9999 to verify their credentials.
5. Confirm your understanding of the fees and commissions you will pay, now and each year. They are due even if your returns are low. If your deferred annuity earns 5% and your fees and charges are 4%, inflation is 3%, your account has lost 2%.

## Plan your financial future yourself and save:

Use the tools in Chapter 2 to complete your plan in an hour. You can have a financial planning firm confirm your plan's strategy. Use one with a set hourly fee only. We will check your plan: Editor@theinsidersguides.com

# How carriers operate annuities:

- Annuities are the most expensive way to obtain tax-deferral.
- Annuities are usually available to age 90 without medical tests.
- Insurers must comply with federal securities law and state insurance regulations.
- Carriers keep your assets separate from theirs with variable annuities. Fixed annuity funds are mingled in their general fund.
- Many sellers charge 1-2% of your account value each year. The money manager charges 1-2% each year. If the insurer earns 7-8% on your money, you may be credited with 4-6%. In addition, you will pay annual policy fees of $50 to $100.

> **Deferred annuities have very high costs.**

- Annuities provide monthly income that you cannot outlive when you "annuitize." However, like most pensions, **the value of the payments fall by half in about 25 years** because of inflation.

# Beware of the misleading claims

1. <u>Charitable gift annuities</u> promise income for life and a memorial for a loved one. The lack of regulation allows anyone to issue fake contracts to accumulate *their* nest egg with the help of independent accountants, agents and planners. You should deal with recognized mutual fund firms or national charities only.

2. **BEWARE**—Financial services firms are targeting you. A recent memo to agents said: "Clients are sitting on hundreds of millions in locked-up IRA's waiting for you [agents] to convert them to annuities. Start Earning Your Huge Commissions Today." This scheme involves buying an annuity "with a 15% 1st year surrender charge and a *15% commission*." **4% is standard!**

3. Another memo to agents and brokers: Earn 17% commission on your annuity sales during seminars structured by mass marketing scheme to get "an average of 120 - 250 affluent seniors every

month." This means that any invitation you receive in the mail offering FREE food for your time from a bank or broker must be treated with the "sleep on it" rule. Don't become a victim of this slick sales method. Tell them you will "sleep on it."

4. A large annuity seller, American Skandia, was sued because it advocated putting its annuity in an IRA. The suit charged American Skandia violated the Securities Act by making misleading statements and omissions in promoting sales of its VAs. The alleged misstatements included an assertion that tax-deferred VAs were suitable for tax-deferred retirement accounts. "Deferred annuities have no place ... in tax-deferred retirement accounts such as IRAs and 401(k)s, which already have these very same tax benefits. The company imposes fees for VAs that in total are two to three times the "normal" commission rates for other investments, such as mutual funds or securities. Purchasers are deprived of up to one-third of their total account value (compared to a regular investment) over the years and are not informed that the circumstances are remote under which the insurance features for which they are paying fees would have any value." "American Skandia believes the claims to be without merit and intends to defend the case vigorously," the spokeswoman says. American Skandia was sold to Prudential.

5. A flexible payment annuity with a guaranteed payout sounds great! You pay $1266 a month from age 50 to 65. You receive $2,000 a month for life. **BAD DEAL** At average market rates of 11%, you could have earned over $500,000 by age 65. That can provide $5,482 per month for 30 years if left in an average stock index fund. This is not guaranteed. However, you have a 125% cushion. On the other hand, the variable annuity only guarantees $2,000 for life or 10 years. If you die before 75, your beneficiary receives only the balance of the $240,000 total required. The insurer keeps the rest--$575,637-$240,000 = $335,637. You will also have income taxes for about 50% of the $24,000 annually. With an index mutual fund, you pay capital gains tax of 5% or 15% depending on your income-tax bracket. Your heirs would pay no tax on the gains, due to "stepped up" status.

6. Bonus 10 Index Annuity offers 10% premium bonus on all premiums received in years 1-5. Sounds good except the seller

does even better----9.5% commission from the policy. **Keep the 9.5% yourself.**

---

**Example of saving up to 83%:**
**Dorothy of New York received an inheritance of $150,000. She has paid all debts and has a great pension. She uses $100,000 to create a tax-free legacy of $300,000 for six grandchildren. She uses $50,000 to buy a TIAA-CREF (rated A++ by AM Best) annuity with expenses of just 0.37%, saving $885 yearly over the industry average expense of 2.14%. That's $8,850 in 10 years.**

---

# EasySheet: Compare features and benefits as well as charges

|  | Company A | Company B | Company C |
|---|---|---|---|
| Premium: Single or Monthly $_____ | | | |
| **Name** | _____ | _____ | _____ |
| Product name | _____ | _____ | _____ |
| Insurer's financial strength rating | _____ | _____ | _____ |
| Surrender charges (% each year) | _____ | _____ | _____ |
| Annual mortality & admin (% per year) | _____ | _____ | _____ |

**Fund management charges** (% per year)

|  | Company A | Company B | Company C |
|---|---|---|---|
| Fixed | _____ | _____ | _____ |
| Money market | _____ | _____ | _____ |
| Stock index | _____ | _____ | _____ |
| Growth | _____ | _____ | _____ |
| Growth and income | _____ | _____ | _____ |
| International stock | _____ | _____ | _____ |
| Bond | _____ | _____ | _____ |
| Other_____ | _____ | _____ | _____ |
| Inter-fund transfer fee | _____ | _____ | _____ |
| Annual policy fee | $ | $ | $ |
| Free withdrawal schedule (% per year) | _____ | _____ | _____ |
| Minimum deposit | $ | $ | $ |
| Additional deposits | $ | $ | $ |
| Seller's commission **(% of deposit)** | _____ | _____ | _____ |

# 10

## The Insider's Guide to Long-term Care Insurance: Do you need it?

**Yes** if,

✓ You are over 65 and have assets <u>under</u> $650,000, or
✓ You have only non-liquid (real estate, business) assets, or
✓ You cannot rely on family to help provide home care help.
✓ Save up to $40,000 over 20 years.

Long-term care insurance is being sold by some sellers using a lot of **misleading** information. The industry bases its sales presentations on these fears:

1. The highest cost of the least needed care: $100,000 or more per year.
2. The fear of being a burden to our families.
3. The fear that we will become destitute.
4. The fear that everyone, including you, will need expensive care.
5. The fear that if we don't buy it now, we will be too sick to buy it later.

The actual situation is quite different. First, 2/3 of us will either never go to a nursing home or will spend less than three months in one. A well-regarded study says that only 13% of women and 4% of men will spend 5+ years in a nursing home: nejm.org/doi/full/10.1056/NEJM199102283240905#t=articleConclusions. Medicaid pays for 49 percent of all long-term care expenditures and almost half of all nursing home care costs. According to LifePlansInc.com, insurance benefits cover only 70% of expenses so having insurance is not enough.

The claim that half of us will need long-term care is misleading. Only 159,000 of the 238 million people under age 65, or less than 0.1 percent, receive nursing-home care. Many of us will receive some kind of care after an operation. Medicare (Part A) and "Medigap" cover some of the costs for the first 100 days after an operation for those over 65.

Consequently, most of the "long-term" care is actually at-home care for a relatively short time. This may not be covered if the policy you purchase has the typical 3 month "waiting" or elimination of claims clause. Benefitscheckup.org.

If we have to, many of us are fine paying $100 a day for an aide to help us after a knee-replacement, for instance. Most of us have family to help us in a temporary situation. No one wants to go to a nursing home for a long period of time. Members who have gone have already given their house or assets away. Many of us may live longer than our parents. Typically, after paying what we can, Medicaid picks up the balance. Most of us will have made some arrangement for our non-essential assets by then. Medicaid pays for most people in long-term custodial care. One analysis shows that "no one has to be poor to receive nursing home care paid for by Medicaid. All anyone needs is a cash flow problem." centerltc.com/pubs/Articles/crisis.htm

Only five percent of people over age 65 have purchased private long-term care insurance, so it is understandable that many insurers want a piece of this lucrative market. Commissions are over 50% of the first year premiums of $1,500 to $10,000, depending on your health and age. In 2010, the average annual premium for a typical policy was $2,539 (longtermcare.gov/) if the policy was purchased at age 65; the premium more than doubled if the policy was purchased at age 75. You can start paying earlier but you may pay for a longer period.

> Almost 1/3 of policies lapse due to increase in costs.

Policies have become more expensive in part because companies have found that their assumptions about usage and costs were wrong. Many insurers have raised their prices by 35% to 45%. Almost a THIRD of policyholders have let their **coverage lapse**! Only 20% of couples under age 60 can afford the premiums today according to the Kaiser Family Foundation.

On the other hand, if you want the **peace of mind** and have the income to afford $2,000 to $3,000 per year per person for 25-30 years ($150,000), then our Insider's suggestions for the purchase are below. Some advisors are against the purchase because their clients have assets to cover the expense if necessary. Prediction techniques are not perfect.

For instance, the cost of the care you are insuring against can average $165,000 in today's dollars. That pays for the average three-year benefit period at an average-priced nursing home.

Check costs in your city at https://www.ltcfeds.com. If you pay $2,000 per person (the current average) for 30 years, you have spent $120,000. If you begin by age 55, you can accumulate $500,000 by the time you need care (83+). See our Insider's Guide to Retirement Spending if this alternative sounds good.

If your idea of peace of mind is **having cash**, self-insure all your long-term needs (health, retirement, emergencies, and legacy) with "assets that grow by themselves." If only one of you needs at-home care for $100 per day for 90 days, your WealthReserve is ahead by $491,000.

Let's assume you want a policy. A typical policy (Genworth with AARP.org discount) costs about $2,600 a year for lifetime benefits of $3,600 per month ($43,200 a year). Even though this benefit does not cover the average cost of nursing home care, the policy does start paying benefits in 30 days. Unfortunately, this policy does not come with an automatic inflation protection. You have to buy additional benefits later, raising the cost when you may not be able to afford it.

If you buy 4 years of coverage, the average, the cost is $1,624. However, you are still going to have to pay for the difference between the cost of care and the insurance benefit. The sellers say that nursing home care can cost $100,000 and you receive only $43,200 a year. So there is a gap of up to $57,000 per year.

Another problem: **inflation**! Inflation will cut your benefit's purchasing power in half by the time you need it. The average age when the policy is put to use is 83. Health-related costs have been increasing at a 5% rate--more than inflation. This means that the difference between what your policy pays and the actual bill will get bigger over time. Clearly, you need a plan.

If you buy a policy, your claims may not be paid. According to a study of 2001 claims data of the National Association of Insurance Commissioners (NAIC), long-term care contracts paid out only 35% of the premiums they took in that year. The contract language protects the insurer, not you. Our LTC **Insider** said that agents do not understand the policies and thus, they use their own interpretation of the marketing materials.

An **example**: GE declined the claim of an 87-year old for assisted-living care in 2002 because her contract said she had to use a facility "licensed" by the "health department." In her state, Massachusetts, all facilities are licensed by the Office of Elder Care Affairs, not by the "health department." So the language of the contract matters!! Ask a elder care lawyer NAELA.com.

Another issue is your insurer's permanence. GE was expected to stay in the long-term care business but they isolated their operations in a separate company called Genworth. John Hancock was expected to stay in business but was purchased by ManuLife (Canada). We don't know if this is a profitable business for ManuLife. According to *Risk & Insurance*, seven insurers have seen return on equity of less than 5%. Many have left the business.

Premiums may keep going up. In 2003, 7 of 10 providers raised the premiums on existing policies—some by over 50%. Companies like C.N.A. raised the price by 15%, then 40% in 2004. GE raised premiums 12% in 2007. According to the Congressional Budget Office CBO.gov, this has lead "many policyholders to cancel their coverage and in all likelihood deterring some potential purchasers from acquiring LTC coverage." **Consumer Reports** found that most states are giving insurers the whole rate increase requested. A man in Texas is suing Standard Life for not telling him about the risks of higher premiums. Adverse selection (healthy people drop coverage) may eventually dry up some insurer's reserves for claimants needing care later.

This leaves us wondering which of the top players in LTC will remain in the business. 88 percent of individual LTCI policies were written by 10 companies. (loma.org) 20 carriers produced 92% of the $1.2 billion of new sales in 2002. Few carriers have NOT raised prices. Some have begun to tighten underwriting on the theory that better management of risk produces profits.

In 2000, GE received 33% of new premiums, Conseco 19%, C.N.A. 8%, and Hancock 7%. AIG, AFLAC, Gerber, TIAA-CREF, Safeco, Principal Life and John Alden discontinued coverage. American Express, Travelers, Fortis, and Transamerica sold their business to others. Policies of CNA were put on the auction block recently. Hancock was purchased by ManuLife (Canada) and Conseco came out of bankruptcy and isolated its LTCi policies in a trust.

Another factor to consider is that the number of us using a nursing home has dropped about 25% from 1994 to 1999. Some cite better health habits and technology. Others mention the hope that genetics may continue the drop in disability rates. New advances in care, like stem cell cures for Alzheimer, make future needs unpredictable. Use this predictor of care needs for an estimate. cumc.columbia.edu/dept/sergievsky/predictor.html

There has been an explosion in the types of alternative living arrangements to meet a diverse set of needs as we get older. New living arrangements may provide better alternatives which may not be covered. Continuing or life-care community living may be attractive alternatives. See SeniorResource.com for housing choices and aging in place planning help. See NewLifeStyles.com, LivHome.com and AoA.gov for alternatives. Germany's system can teach us some lessons.
http://assets.aarp.org/rgcenter/il/2007_19_usgerman_ltc.pdf

## Which benefits do you need?

1. Skilled and intermediate care cost the most. Definitions: aim-aiu.com/GLOSSARY.htm
2. Qualification for care determined by your OWN doctor, not the insurer's.
3. "Facility only" and "90-day elimination" (waiting) period lowers your premium. Only 14.4 percent of closed long-term care insurance claims lasted longer than 24 months. emaxhealth.com/105/4272.html
4. "Compound inflation" rider prevents benefit short-fall in 20 years. 'Waiver of premium' when using benefits. Re-load benefit period after triggers are met.
5. Policy that covers your conditions: treatment that your family *can't* provide.

The type of coverage you need depends on your age and retirement plans. If your budget cannot sustain the increases in premium for 20 or more years, it is better to self-insure. Almost half of nursing-home stays last three months or less. If stays are preceded by hospitalization, Medicare.gov may cover you after age 65. See below. Check your "medigap" coverage benefits. Some members have found savings of $1,000 for the same benefits from one provider over another. Some life insurance policies offer options to pay for care with a LTC rider. businessweek.com 5/2/05
More than one-third of nursing home stays last one year or longer. Only 14.4 percent of closed long-term care insurance claims lasted longer than 24 months. Only 8% of 70-year-old claimants will need care for more than 5 years. (kiplinger.com/magazine/archives/2006/05/ltc.html) It is the costly

longer stay that may be the devastating financial blow that you may want to insure against. If you want peace of mind, buy "facilities only" coverage for 2 years so that the most likely catastrophic expense is covered. AARP says that the compound inflation rider is the most important part of any policy. Also, buy a policy that allows your ***own doctor*** to certify that you qualify for benefits.

If you can allocate at least $160,000 of your assets to your reserve, you probably don't need a policy, according to Consumer Reports.org. This is the amount that the average stay in the average nursing home costs TODAY. If your stay is longer, you may have to use the rest of your discretionary assets. In most states, your spouse does not have to become destitute for you to use Medicaid. A healthy spouse can keep your home, car, and retirement income. A healthy spouse can keep half of the remaining assets up to $109,560. estateattorney.com/elderlaw-articles/insurance-longtermcare.html

## What to avoid

✓ Policies with hospitalization-first requirement; shorter waiting period; no medical questions.
✓ Non-renewable; "return of premium;" refund at death; "low-ball" initial premiums and "nonforfeiture" policies. Aim-aiu.com/Glossary
✓ "Periodic purchase" option. Compounding helps benefit amount match inflation rate.
✓ Buying early: $1,625 at age 50 costs $168,949 by age 83. Buy at age 70 ($7,575) costs only $98,475 by age 83 with less chance of increases. Play the odds depending on your family history.

Avoid buying a policy you cannot afford for 30 years given the inevitable premium increases. Policies without full inflation protection of 5% compounded will leave you with a shortfall every day. If $100 a day is almost enough for coverage today, it will be worth less than $50 in 20 years. Avoid period "purchase options" policies. Avoid "nonforfeiture" riders.

Avoid plans that try to cover all needs. If you need assisted-living care, make sure that you don't have to go to the hospital first. Avoid benefit "triggers" that require the insurer's doctor to agree. Avoid the requirement that you need to fail many Activities of Daily Living, ADL's, to get benefits. One ADL, bathing, should be the trigger to receive benefits. Make sure the premium quote is on par with other insurers. New insurers don't have claim experience and price policies poorly.

## How much coverage to buy?

NONE. Self-insure with a Self-Insurance **Wealth Reserve**™ for the same price. If your family members are willing to provide assistance in your own home, modify living space to make daily necessities easier. Women need care more often than men do. Depending on your income and assets, a plan to use a pool of resources by the extended family may offer the best compromise for older family members. Determine needs from past-year medical necessities. Anticipate major expenses. Planning and family discussions assure affordable and acceptable alternatives. Talk about 'what ifs.' Read "The Senior Solution: A Family Guide to Keeping Seniors Home For Life!"

Pick a "facility only" policy with the longest waiting period (deductible) you can afford. Check exclusions and pre-existing condition rules. Explore joint insured discount. Pick 2 year coverage. emaxhealth.com/105/4272.html

Choose optional coverage with care—premium refund options may not work. Anticipate price hikes. Care costs can rise faster (8%) than inflation rider (5%).

If you have coverage from your current employer, check for portability and inflation protection.
The wording of insurance policies is confusing and unclear. Ask, "What happens" in typical claims like hip replacement recovery or can't bathe or dress yourself.

Saved $120,000
Mr. and Mrs. K., in their 60's, compared LTC with a joint annuity that had a LTC waiver for their needs. The annual cost was $2,000 each for a LTC policy. $50,000 annuity costs 2.5% annually but taxes must be paid by heirs if not used for LTC. Wealth Reserve is tax-friendly now and heirs pay no tax on accumulation of $1/2 million if not used.

Make a plan that matches your lifestyle. This means deciding by age 65 whether you want to self-insure or buy insurance for part of the costs. Assess your need for long-term care and your resources. Discuss your plans with family and unbiased advisors (not sales people). Use the experience of others who have been through this. Get advice at Eldercare.gov (800.677.1116), Caremanager.org (520.881.8008), and Naela.com (520.881.4005).

Once you make a plan, do the research necessary to understand your options: policy coverage can vary from company to company and policy benefits usually require additional funds to fill the gaps. Compare prices from the largest sellers with our EasySheet page 13. Use the information in the Fed's Shopper's Guide ltcfeds.com/documents/files/NAIC_Shoppers_Guide.pdf to understand which coverage you want to pay for yourself.

# Best value

✓ A "Self-insurance" **Wealth Reserve**™ created over 25 years versus policy premiums payable until death. $2,000 ($166 monthly) in a stock market mutual fund becomes $300,000 in 25 years. See our Insider's Guide to Retirement Spending.

✓ If buying a policy, pick facility care, 90 waiting, compound inflation, renewal guaranteed, with "pre-existing" condition. Make sure the nursing homes in your area are covered.

✓ 2-year benefit for female allows family to adjust to new reality and is cost effective. Shared care and spouse discounts are available.

✓ FIRST: discuss and plan for emergency and contingencies with family.

✓ Check facilities at consumerreports.org, medicare.gov, state health officials (naic.org/state_web_map.htm) and local non-profit hospitals social workers.

Your best value is to have the cash to extend the lifestyle you want, as long as you want it. The future of medical techniques to prolong life is not predictable. It is your choice to use your cash for insurance or for **staying out of a nursing home** as long as possible. *ConsumerReports.org* reviewed 47 policies in 2003. They concluded that "for most people, long-term-care insurance is too risky and too expensive." Plus, the IRS helps you pay for home remodeling if you need it.

**If self-insurance is not for you**, buy "facility-only" coverage so that you are not wiped-out. At 65, a healthy woman can buy three years of care after waiting 90 days for about $1,500. Ask the insurer to debit your checking account automatically so the policy won't lapse. Keep a "medigap" policy. LTC premium might be tax-deductible. Make sure you can afford this premium and the increases for over 25 years. The average age of initial use is 83 and climbing.

Most people now in nursing homes need help taking a bath. Make sure this is one of the trigger points in your policy. Find one that allows your doctor to make the decisions. Most nursing home stays last less than 3 years. If you have to stay longer, the nursing home will usually accept Medicaid. The government (CBO.gov) says that "Medicaid serves as an alternative form of insurance for people who do not have private coverage and who are impaired for a significant period."

Planning for this stage of life is hard for most people. Those who say they planned well established their wishes with their family in advance, sometimes using legal means. For instance, they gave away their valuable assets to family or a trust in advance. One member gave their home to their kids but they can't sell it until later. Another member is going to use their paid-off home as their "LTC insurance". Others have decided to put their assets in a trust. Build your plan around your benefits from Medicare and Medicaid. See below. Consult ElderLawAnswers.com about new rules on home equity. elderlawanswers.com/elder_info/elder_article.asp?id=2751

## How and where to buy

Compare quotes at Aarp.org (866 660.4117), LTCq.net (800-587-3279). You give information about yourself and a seller contacts you.
Compare plans of your employer, association, fraternal or religious group to the federal (ltcfeds.com) plan.
Contact a specialist through AALTCI. (aaltci.org): You can find a seller in your area for a face-to-face meeting.
Consult an elder attorney (naela.com) if your estate is complicated.

Usually, the carriers with the largest number of policies are the most likely to be around when you need them in 20 or 30 years. All federal and military workers can buy long term care insurance. John Hancock and MetLife provide LTC through Long Term Care Partners (ltcfeds.com). The web site contains extensive information about the price and application questions so you can see what is involved. Some members have found the policy over-priced. Compare the NY Times complaint investigations. medicalnewstoday.com/articles/66208.php

A few states (CT, NY, IN, CA) have recognized that we don't want to become destitute in order to pay for long term care insurance. They offer Partnership http://www.nyspltc.org/ policies that protect a certain level of assets if you buy a policy. However, it is not clear whether this arrangement works for everyone. Compare costs and benefits with our EasySheet below.

Check the nursing facility you are considering. Some seek to take only those with private insurance. Unfortunately, what you pay for does not always match what you get. Services and standards are not closely regulated in some states. Even the states with great regulations don't always keep up with nursing home operations or management. Ask the ltcombudsman.org for help.

The Consumers Union has surveyed the problem and has a 2002 Watch List. consumersunion.org/health/nursing-tab1.htm#table1vv
They suggest you obtain the state survey on your facility from the facility itself. You want to keep close tabs on the facility. After you oversee the initial care planning that all facilities are required to do, follow up at each visit to make sure the plan is used. Join the home's "family council" so that your concerns are taken seriously.


## Critical policy elements

1.  If policy renewal isn't guaranteed, you may not have coverage when you need it.
2.  If you are in good health, medical questions save you money. If not, see **Bad Health**.
3.  Select a company with high financial strength ("A") so benefits are there in 20-30 years.
4.  Automatic premium payments from your credit card or bank prevents policy lapse.
5.  Your application is part of the contract. You and carrier (not

agent) must sign all changes.

# Bad health?

✓  If you have a major illness, your employer, association or union may offer a group policy that doesn't require tests. Carriers specialize and independent agents can help you with specific medical problems.

✓  Seek a group policy if your health will disqualify you from individual coverage. A group plan may have fewer benefits but you will have some peace of mind. Check employer plans for portability and premium rate, if you leave.

In recent years, some insurers have tightened underwriting in order to reduce the possibility of higher than expected claims. There are specialists who may help you find some coverage. However, be prepared for higher premiums in the future. The carrier can raise premiums if they are raised for everyone in your underwriting class.

Ultimately, you may find that you have no choice but to self-insure. In short, this means you must buy "assets that grow by themselves" to create a **Wealth Reserve**™. If you need long-term care in your home or other facility, you can pay as you go. If you made a plan to leave some assets to your family or charity, there are several methods that accomplish this. When your **Wealth Reserve**™ is depleted, your care will be taken over by Medicaid if needed.

---

**Example of shopping:** Mr. D. wanted quality care for Mrs D, if needed. He called GE, Hancock, Travelers, C.N.A., UNUM agents for a $100/day 3-year benefit policy, 90 day waiting period, standard non-cancelable, 5% compounded inflation adjustment. Lowest cost was $1,519 annually at age 65, or $30,380 by age 85. Mr and Mrs. D. have comfortable pension and health care.

---

# Your Rights and Benefits

The National Association of Insurance Commissioners policy standards:

At least one year of nursing home or home health care coverage, including intermediate and custodial care. Nursing home or home health care benefits not be limited primarily to skilled care.

Coverage for Alzheimer's disease, should the policyholder develop it after purchasing the policy.

An inflation protection option. The policy should offer a choice among: automatically increasing the initial benefit level on an annual basis, a guaranteed right to increase benefit levels periodically without providing evidence of insurability, or covering a specific percentage of actual or reasonable charges.

An "outline of coverage" that systematically describes the policy's benefits, limitations, and exclusions, and also allows you to compare it with others. A long-term care insurance *shopper's guide* that helps you decide whether long-term care insurance is appropriate

A guarantee that the policy cannot be terminated because you get older or suffer deterioration in physical or mental health.

The right to return the policy within 30 days after you have purchased the policy and to receive a premium refund.

No requirement that policyholders: first be hospitalized in order to receive nursing home benefits or home health care benefits, first receive skilled nursing home care before receiving intermediate or custodial nursing home care, first receive nursing home care before receiving benefits for home health care.

Medicare provides nursing and home and hospice care:

You have been hospitalized 3 days prior to needing skilled-nursing care, and a doctor certifies that you need it. Skilled-nursing-facility expenses for 20 days. Then you are responsible for a co-payment (now $105 a day). Medicare ceases payments after 100 days per benefit period. (A benefit period begins the first time you are hospitalized and ends only after you have been out of the hospital for 60 days.)

You are homebound, under a doctor's care, require skilled-nursing care, and require a part-time home-health-aide and medical services. All medical services are paid. Skilled-nursing and home-health-aide services for no more than 8 hours per day, or a maximum of 28 hours a week. Eighty percent of medical equipment such as hospital beds and walkers.

A doctor certifies that you have 6 months or less to live. Two 90-day periods of care followed by an unlimited number of 60-day periods. All expenses for nursing and medical services, supplies, counseling, and home-health and homemaker services in a Medicare-approved hospice. Drugs and bereavement costs. Five percent of the cost of outpatient drugs, up to $5 per prescription, may be charged. medicare.gov/Nursing/Payment.asp

Medicaid Conditions

You meet a state-determined poverty level and certain health-related criteria. Generally, you may keep only the house, furniture, a car, a burial plot and funeral funds, your IRA (some states) and half of your family assets up to $109,560 (2009).

Coverage includes room, board, nursing care, and social activities in the nursing facility. http://www.estateattorney.com/

## EasySheet  Find out if you have the best coverage options

|  | Company A | Company B | Company C |
|---|---|---|---|

Name _____

Premium: ☐Annual ☐Quarter ☐Month

**Nursing home, assisted living facility, home, adult day care, "informal" care**
Glossary http://www.aim-aiu.com/glossary.htm

| | Company A | Company B | Company C |
|---|---|---|---|
| **$60 daily for 4 years; wait 30 days:** | $ _____ | $ _____ | $ _____ |
| $120 daily for 4 years; wait 90 days: | $ _____ | $ _____ | $ _____ |
| $200 daily for 4 years; wait 90 days: | $ _____ | $ _____ | $ _____ |
| $200 daily for life; wait 90 days: | $ _____ | $ _____ | $ _____ |
| $200 daily for life; wait 365 days: | $ _____ | $ _____ | $ _____ |
| Duplicate coverage for spouse: | $ _____ | $ _____ | $ _____ |
| **Total Premium** | $ _____ | $ _____ | $ _____ |

### Checklist of valuable benefits

| | Company A | Company B | Company C |
|---|---|---|---|
| Couple discount | ___ | ___ | ___ |
| No pre-existing limitations | ___ | ___ | ___ |
| Family medical history good | ___ | ___ | ___ |
| All sickness and accidents covered | ___ | ___ | ___ |
| Waiver of premium | ___ | ___ | ___ |
| Compound inflation increases automatic | ___ | ___ | ___ |
| Waiting period once in lifetime | ___ | ___ | ___ |
| Non-cancelable/renewable | ___ | ___ | ___ |
| Alzheimer's covered | ___ | ___ | ___ |
| No prior hospital stay | ___ | ___ | ___ |
| Own doctor certified 2 of 6 ADL's | ___ | ___ | ___ |

# 11

## The Insider's Guide to Wealth Transfer:
## Create a family legacy

✓      You have money beyond your retirement income needs, and
✓      You have provided for final expenses in your Will, and
✓      You want to provide funds to family at death free of taxes.

### Ways to transfer wealth
*This is not legal advice. See a qualified estate attorney.*

1.      If you leave an IRA, pension, or **annuity**, your beneficiary may have to pay <u>federal income taxes</u> on the gain. If your estate value will be **over** $5,000,000 it may have tax to pay.*
2.      If you leave a mutual funds, securities, or other assets that have gone up in value, your beneficiary will **NOT** have to pay federal <u>income taxes on the gains. Your estate may have to pay tax.</u>* <u>http://taxes.about.com/od/capitalgains/a/CapitalGainsTax_4.htm</u>
3.      Life insurance can provide a legacy at death without income taxes. Pick one with no commission, annual fee, surrender charges, or loads. The estate may have tax to pay.*

*Estate value is assets less debts at death. The portion not taxed <u>changes</u> annually. <u>IRS.gov</u>

You can transfer the amount and type of assets that your plan calls for. One member had an adequate pension and supplemental income so that she bought a single payment life policy for $50,000. The benefit of about $150,000 would be split equally to her four grandchildren as her legacy. She did this outside of her will and probate. The grandchildren or their guardians will have access to the funds within 30 days. She does not have a big estate so the policy will not create an estate tax problem.

     Another method of accomplishing a legacy is the way John and Liz did. (box below) Investing $100,000 in a low-cost tax-managed mutual fund for 15 years may mean leaving $600,000 (market average rate is 12%) to the children. At death the exact value is distributed according to their Will. If their estate totals less than the federal exemption, the $600,000 is passed with no estate tax. The benefit of this method is that John and Liz can use the assets for long-term care, if needed, and the heirs will pay no federal income tax.

You want to avoid leaving a <u>deferred</u> annuity untapped. Tax on the earnings is deferred and, over time a $100,000 may grow to over $500,000. At death, the named beneficiaries will owe income tax at *their* income tax rate. The <u>legacy</u> could be much less than planned. Instead, you can "annuitize" monthly income from your annuity and buy a tax-managed mutual fund. Avoid <u>selling</u> your annuity for cash. businessweek.com/magazine/content/06_19/b3983097.htm

---

**Save 90% on Wealth Transfer**
John and Liz, 65, of West Virginia had $100,000 in accounts producing income they had to pay tax on. They have great pensions and health care. If they don't need the money they want their **3 kids** to have it. Both chose Vanguard's tax-managed funds with expenses of just 0.17% vs 1.52% <u>industry average</u>, saving $1,503 annually. Each child may receive over $100,000 tax-FREE.

---

An IRA left to any person including your spouse can be rolled over without <u>tax</u> problems. Your spouse can use your IRA like you did —pay tax when you withdraw funds. If the named beneficiary is a person, there are several options, including stretching the payout over many years. First, each beneficiary (if more than one) should take their part right away. Do NOT put the IRA directly into your name. This makes the inherited IRA fully **taxable** in one year. The financial firm must keep your name and FBO your beneficiary on the account to let it grow tax-deferred. They need to make withdrawals every year -- withdrawing the entire amount either within five years or "stretching" it over *your* life expectancy. Your beneficiary can exchange the assets for any type they like inside the account. irs.gov/publications/p590/ch01.html#d0e949

Your beneficiary can liquidate the IRA. Tax is due at a higher tax bracket usually. If your beneficiary does not need or want the money, it can be given to someone else who can use the tax-deferral benefits. However, you must do this before death by naming a contingent beneficiary. The primary beneficiary could then choose to 'disclaim,' or give up control of, the IRA while the estate is being settled. The account would then pass to your contingent beneficiary.

Leaving an unused IRA (mandated withdrawals at 70.5 years) to heirs makes the IRS's mouth water. The IRS can assess a 50 percent penalty (Irahelp.com) on the amount that should already have been taken out. There are taxes to pay also. Finally, the amount that the designated beneficiary is required to withdraw from an inherited IRA can vary greatly so check with your tax person. Most advisors are not experts at IRA distributions. Find one with special training at Irahelp.com/.

As a grandparent, you can contribute five years' worth of gifts ($13,000 per year per kid) to a 529 education plan in one year without gift taxes. irs.gov/pub/irs-pdf/p950.pdf Your state may limit the amount you can deduct each year. You still control it. If one grandchild doesn't use it, you can switch beneficiaries. Contribution limits are high. Money in a grandparent-owned 529 generally isn't included as an asset on financial aid forms. You can move more money out of your estate by paying part of the tuition bills, too, as long as you pay the school directly.

WARNING: This Guide offers suggestions on how to fund your legacy yourself. This Guide suggests how to establish a tax-free legacy for your family or charity. Before you change your current accounts, make certain that the alternative plan is in place. Do not cancel any accounts before you check with your lawyer about your alternative arrangement. Start your **Wealth Reserve**™.

If your estate value will exceed the exemption (IRS.gov) in the future, make a plan that lowers your estate by changing the owner of your assets or giving your assets to your family now. For instance, one member had a large insurance policy death benefit (not cash value) which would have put his estate over the exemption. The member transferred 'ownership' of the policy to his four adult children. Each offspring cannot sell the policy by themselves and their share of the death benefit does not put them close to their own exemption limit if they should die first. The member continues to pay the premium via gifts. Each child will receive 1/4 of the death benefit.

# How much should you transfer?

You should transfer as much as your plan designates for estate tax and beneficiary income tax purposes. Certain assets that have grown in value pass to beneficiaries without federal income tax due. These include life insurance death benefits, real property, securities, and personal property, as long as you don't sell them previously. Other account assets with tax-deferral benefits like IRAs, annuities, and pensions pass with the same taxation as ordinary income. All may be included in your estate and taxed at up to 46%.

Before making plans for a legacy, make sure you will not need supplemental retirement income or emergency health care funds. A strategy that provides for both contingencies is the one that grows assets at low taxation and is distributed to the heirs without income tax to them. If the funds are needed for an emergency, they are readily available at low rates. The tax-managed growth funds used by our members John and Liz (box above) do this efficiently and at low cost. Historically, the funds compound at 10% over periods greater than 10 years.

# What to avoid

✓      Letting others decide for you. Our members take control of their futures.
✓      Banks, agents, and brokers have targeted the $ billions to be inherited by all of us.
✓      Not making a comprehensive financial plan for all your assets.

Avoid buying financial products without a plan of what you want to accomplish with your money. Sales people practice all their lives to give you a reason to buy their favorite product NOW. It is like going to the store without a list—you will buy anything on impulse and then you can't take it back. No one likes to admit they made a mistake. It is hard to get your money back.

Every banker, agent, broker and scam artist knows the game—meet with the folks with the money: YOU. All financial firms push annuities today. Sellers make 4% to 19% (bankrate.com) of the deposit in exchange for a promise that you can earn a higher return than a CD. If you don't need the money now, a fixed rate annuity probably sounds good. But, you can't get your money back easily and as rates climb, your rate will lag the current rate. The problem is that your heirs will have to pay income tax on the annuity.

A financial plan helps you make sure your money does what you want it to do. A sales person is not trained to give you the low-cost alternatives. Our Insider worked with sales people in a Wall Street securities firm and banks for 20 years. He found that brokers and bankers concentrate on selling only three products beneficial to the firm. Our Insider noted that the sales people do not sell the best product for your situation or even the products with the lowest costs to you, the buyer. They sell what fits their firm's sales strategy. It is like going to your local hardware store and buying the top-of-the-line gas grill when the same grill is available at 50% off at the "big box" stores. You lose.

## Best value

✓ "Direct" providers don't have the expenses of field agents and fancy buildings.
✓ Products with total expenses under 0.30% with no surrender, commission, annual fee, loads, etc.
✓ Best products grow tax-advantaged now and pass tax-free at death.

The best value is usually a quality product without the annual fees or commissions or surrender charges or loads or sales pressure from using a sales person. Using the information in this Guide, you can buy DIRECT from the top rated financial providers just like the professionals do. The money you save and invest year after year can enhance your legacy considerably.

Just as important, you control the future of your financial life. With our Guides you have more alternatives that benefit you not the sales person. You gain peace of mind from understanding how to use your funds to accomplish your goals for current expenses and your legacy. Tax-managed mutual funds from Vanguard or T. Rowe Price have low annual fees and no commissions.

For instance, one member has kept 40% of her assets in stocks, 40% bonds, and 20% short-term investments even during her retirement to assure her family will meet their lifetime income goals. This allocation of assets was tested in hundreds of market simulations by Troweprice.com. The Retirement Income Calculator allows you to test different combinations of assets to see which will produce your monthly income goal. This calculator is useful because the test is done while the calculator increases the income amount to keep pace with inflation over the rest of your life. See The Insider's Guide to Retirement Spending above.

This member has a legal will that passes the assets to family heirs with no income taxes due at death. Beneficiaries can use all the assets for any purpose—without having to pay income taxes on the gains. They can build their own **Wealth Reserve**™.

A widowed member with 5 grandchildren wished to provide each with a gift at her death. She was quite wealthy and the life insurance death benefit would have increased the estate tax bill. She purchased a single payment policy making her 2 sons the owners and their kids the beneficiaries. Her estate will not have to pay tax on the face amount and her grandchildren will share the $1,000,000 tax-free death benefit.

## How and where to buy

1.      Tax-managed/efficient funds: Vanguard.com (**877.662.7447**) and TRowePrice.com (**800.225.5132**). $10,000 becomes $25,000 in 10 years at 10%. The funds grow with little current tax and low expenses. Your *will* designates heirs who pay no income tax. If you need the funds, the gains are taxed at lower rates—5% or 15%.

2.      Whole life insurance creates an immediate legacy:

SBLIUSA.com (**877.725.4872**) and WesternSouthernLife.com (**866.832.7719**). At age 60, a $25,000 legacy costs about $33 per month. At age 75, a $20,000 legacy costs about $165 per month.

3.        Single payment or modified whole life buys the benefit with one payment. SBLIUSA.com (**877.725.4872**) and WesternSouthernLife.com (**866.832.7719**). At age 65, a female non-smoker can buy about $66,000 in death benefits for about $20,000 without fluid tests.

4.        Donor-advised funds let you obtain your deduction immediately and follow your instructions after death. Fidelity and Vanguard have made it easy. Give, deduct, and advise which charity to support. This is the least expensive way to reduce your estate.

5.        Trusts are designed to fit specific needs to transfer wealth and control taxation. Living in your home after giving it away or making a reverse mortgage for more income are options. Giving away property now that has increased in value can provide tax deductions and an income for life. Ask an elder lawyer (naela.org).

Your time horizon determines your choice of financial instruments. If your life expectancy is more than 10 years, you can maintain control of your assets for emergencies and, at the same time, grow your legacy for your family using stock funds. You pay little income tax now as your tax-managed mutual funds grow. Your family pays NO income tax when the funds are bequeathed to them in your Will.

If you want to provide a living gift to your grandchildren now, you can contribute $13,000 per year to their 529 college fund. You can give any number of people $13,000 (2011) each year without jeopardizing your estate tax exemption. Use our Insider's Guide to Education Funding to save up to $20,000 in account fees.

You can make annual gifts of up to $5,000 to a young person's Roth IRA. They will have a tax-**FREE** fund for later. They must have matching income amounts from any source to eligible. Check Chapter 2 of IRS.gov Pub 590 for complete guidelines on opening a Roth IRA.

> Their
> **WEALTH**
> **RESERVE**
> is your Gift
> of a
> Lifetime

be

Another strategy is to buy one life insurance policy for all your named beneficiaries outside your Will and probate. You can add or subtract names to the list. You can purchase the policy with one payment or periodic payments for the rest of your life. Annual premiums of $4302 buys a $100,000 legacy at age 70 for a non-smoking female. westernsouthernlife.com/products/quote_27.asp

Single premium life policy creates an immediate legacy with one payment (SBLI.com). Some fraternal organizations and SBLI offer policies with low fees and commissions for their members. Some low-cost insurers (TIAA-CREF.org, USAA.com) offer universal life. You may find it convenient to use part of your funds to buy life insurance and part to buy a tax-advantaged growth mutual fund. In that case, you are making sure of a legacy NOW and providing for a potentially bigger legacy in the future.

Deferred annuities offer you, NOT your heirs, the benefits of tax-deferred growth. Unfortunately, your heirs get a big tax bill if you don't begin using these annuities before your will is read. Deferred annuities should be annuitized and the periodic payments

> Tax deferral of unrealized capital gains are considered an interest-free loan from the government that can be paid back at the investor's choosing.
>
> Warren Buffett, renowned investor.

used to buy a tax-FREE legacy for your family. You can also give them to a charity for a current deduction and income to buy a tax-FREE legacy. pcalc.ptec.com/hosts/989357365/CGA/

## The critical elements

1. Select a company with high financial strength and experience with the product.
2. Make sure the product's strengths and weaknesses fit your plan.
3. Balance inflation risk with market risk. The annual fees rob you of the power of compounding.
4. Know the salesperson. Check the FINRA.org (800.289.9999) and insurance department (NAIC.org).
5. Confirm your understanding of the annual fees and commissions you will pay.

# Chart your financial future

✓       Your union or association or mutual fund firm may offer fee-based planning services at low cost.

✓       You can complete your own plan using this book. Chapter 2 shows you how to buy "assets that grow by themselves." It assures you will accomplish your goals. Keep a record with this CD: http://store.kiplinger.com/family_records_info.html

✓       Find a Fee-only Planner in your area. NAPFA.org. Learn more about financial planning FREE: ocw.uci.edu/courses/course.aspx?id=12

Seek a fee-only planner if you don't feel confident you can gain control of your financial life using our Guides. Some members have done their plan and then received a confirmation of what they have done by having a professional at one of the mutual fund firms check it. This may cost nothing. Check with Vanguard.com or Troweprice.com for details.

A financial plan needs to be revised AFTER retirement in order to make sure you have enough income for the rest of your life. Many people are living to age 90 or more and need an income for 30 years. Since inflation of 3% cuts the purchasing power of income by 50% in 25 years, we need to plan how funds are invested to keep pace with our needs. Check our Insider's Guide to Buying an Annuity above to see why this darling of the industry may NOT be right for you.

In a real sense, we all need to keep our investment plan working AFTER retirement begins. Many independent people keep about half of our assets in stock funds through retirement so that they can maintain the same income purchasing power that they had when they began retirement. Many people keep working past 65 in order to supplement their declining income.

Since we don't know how long we will need an income in retirement, we need to plan for both--income to live on for perhaps 30 years or more and a legacy for our family's benefit without taxes. You can use our Insider's Guide to Retirement Spending above to make sure you have enough. Once you have done that, you can relax.

Many financial advisors claim to provide the expertise to manage your portfolio for life. However, there are no guarantees (except the fees). Things happen. Even if you are wealthy, an illness or accident can severely curtail your ability to retain enough assets to live at the same standard for life and leave a legacy too. See our Insider's Guide to Long-term Care Insurance above. The best each of us can do is to make a plan we understand so we stick with it.

---

**A legacy can be created in many ways:**

1.      Financial assets in a taxable account. Heir pays no income tax. Value is 'stepped-up.'
2.      Financial assets in a tax-deferred account. Heir pays income tax.
3.      Financial assets in a Roth IRA account. Heir pays no income tax.
4.      Financial assets in an insurance policy. Heir pays no income tax.
5.      Financial assets in a trust. Heir pays no income tax. Trust does.

---

Stock mutual funds work the hardest for you and your heirs

1.      Tax-managed and growth index mutual funds grow with little current taxation.
2.      Index funds usually have lower expenses since they buy and hold market securities.
3.      The size of your legacy depends on time not on what you buy. (Since 1976, stock index funds have averaged over 10% per year. https://personal.vanguard.com/us/funds/snapshot? FundId=0040&FundIntExt=INT)
4.      Taxes on the accumulation of value are payable only if you sell the funds. Tax on the gains is at a more favorable rate. There are NO INCOME TAXES due when passed to your heirs. Designate "Payable on Death" beneficiary to avoid probate.
5.      Funds accumulated inside a Roth IRA for 5 years are tax-FREE.

6.      Funds are subject to estate tax and the probate process.

## Annuities, IRAs and Pensions

1.      There is a maximum contribution, mandatory distribution, income tax payable by your heirs.
2.      There are surrender charges, fees, mortality expenses, commissions.
3.      There are no medical questions, blood tests, doctor statements, MIB.com reports.
4.      Subject to estate tax but not subject to probate process.

## Life Insurance

1.      There is a maximum contribution, no mandatory distribution, no income tax payable by your heirs.
2.      There are surrender charges, annual fees, mortality expenses, commissions.
3.      There are medical questions, blood tests, doctor statements, MIB.com reports. (Some small policies have no fluid tests.)
4.      Subject to estate tax but not subject to probate process. Check for an unclaimed policy at MIB.com.

## Trust assets

1.      There is no maximum contribution, no mandatory distribution, and no income tax payable by your heirs.
2.      There are initial costs and annual fees.
3.      Trust pays income taxes but not subject to probate process.

Long-term investment funds let you keep control of your assets.

# Wealth Transfer Checklist

>>Identify sources of emergency funds. Money market? Home equity line?

>>Pay down all debt. Your home equity loan approval provides extra security.

>>Protect your family and assets using TheInsidersGuides to save up to $3,000 per year.

>>Tap into all your retirement accounts: 401K, IRA, annuity and pensions. They are taxable to heirs if unused. Use the excess income to fund a TAX-FREE legacy—insurance or Roth IRA or POD account.

>>BEWARE: deferred annuities pass with income tax owed at the beneficiary's rate. Your insurance, annuities and IRAs are assets and may trigger estate tax.

>>Excess funds can establish a legacy for family and charities now (scholarship in your name?). There are many Wealth Transfer strategies. If your estate value will exceed the $1,000,000 exclusion, see an elder lawyer (naela.org) now.

>>Budget your retirement income and expense, including vacations and property changes.

>>If you have not provided for final expenses and instructions, do so now. Funerals.org's Consumers Alliance have information on funeral costs and pre-paying it. Pre-payment may fail. Leave enough funds in your Will with instructions about final events. Your funeral home may go bankrupt.

>>There are tax-managed mutual funds that limit current income in order to grow with little current income taxes. At death, the accumulated value can be passed FREE of federal income taxes, unlike your 401Ks, IRAs, annuities and pensions.

>>You can create a legacy instantly by buying life insurance. The death benefit can be passed without income taxes or probate. Insurance owned by family members or a trust removes it from your estate value.

>>Create and fund your buy/sell business succession plan to avoid dissolution to pay tax or split the firm. This is most effectively done by business-owned life insurance.

>>You need an estate lawyer if you have complicated family ties, a large estate, gifting your home, a business or a family legacy.

# Assets can be controlled in many ways. Consult an attorney

**Joint tenant with survivorship**
Assets passed to the 'survivor'
Assets passed at death FREE of income tax
Avoids probate

**Tenant by entirety**
Assets passed to the spouse not creditors
Assets passed at death FREE    of income tax
Avoids probate

**Tenants in common**
Asset share passed by owner's will
Assets passed at death FREE of income tax
Probate according to owner's state

**Community property**
Assets acquired by either belong to both
Assets passed at death to beneficiary        of will
Probate according to owner's state
Assets before marriage need protection

**Revocable living trust**
Give property to trust
You are trustee
Third party guidance
Trust buys future assets
Avoids probate
Controls businesses
Keep assets private
Legacy simplified
Initial costs to transfer assets

Annual costs
Tax same as individual

**Charitable trusts**
Avoid income, gains, and estate taxes
Asset cannot be reclaimed
Income for life arrangement

**Durable power of attorney**
Person acts for you when you can't
Accident victim
Incompetence

**Accounts for others**
Living trust
Assets passed at death FREE of income tax
Avoids probate

**Family limited partnership**
Assets shifted to children
Tax on accumulation reduced
Assets control retained
Buy/sell agreement for liquidation

**Other strategies (see appropriate lawyer)**
Family-owned life insurance
Business-owned life insurance
Business-owned assets
Limited liability companies
Gifting assets
Your Foundation (DAF)

# EasySheet      **Leave More to Your Family**

**Current Financial Assets**

|  |  | John & Liz | Yours |
|---|---|---|---|
| Money Market Accounts | income tax now | $ 4,000 | $_____ |
| Certificates of Deposits | income tax now | $ 5,000 | $_____ |
| Mutual Funds (bonds) | income tax now | $ 100,000 | $_____ |
| IRAs, Annuities | tax owed by heirs | $ 15,000 | $_____ |
| Life Insurance |  | $ 0 | $_____ |
| Other |  | $ 0 | $_____ |
| Total Legacy now |  | $ 124,000 | $_____ |

**New Re-Allocated Portfolio (legacy value)**

|  |  | John & Liz | Yours |
|---|---|---|---|
| Money Market Accounts | no tax owed by heirs | $ 4,000 | $_____ |
| Certificates of Deposits | to insurance | $ 0 | $_____ |
| Mutual Funds (stock tax-managed) | no tax owed by heirs | $ 417,725 | $_____ |
| IRAs, Annuities | to insurance | $ 0 | $_____ |
| Life Insurance ($20,000 premium) | no tax owed by heirs | $ 66,000 | $_____ |
| Other |  | $ 0 | $_____ |
| Total Legacy in 15 years* |  | **$ 487,725** | **$_____** |
| Increase in Estate Value using tax-managed stock fund |  | **$ 317,725** | **$_____** |
| Increase using Single Pay Life |  | **$ 46,000** | **$_____** |

*Legacy values include purchase of Ultimate II, Jackson National Life policy and Vanguard tax-managed Capital Appreciation fund. It assumes no withdrawals, returns reinvested and 10% average annual return compounded for 15 years. Other assets have been given to family at under $12,000 per year. No estate tax.

# 12

## The Insider's Guide for Women: Protect Your Financial Health

✓ Women are better investors than men but they aren't getting rich.

✓ Women control family spending but families are falling in debt.

✓ A woman's average retirement income will be 56 percent less than a man's income.

✓ Women lose over $600,000 in earnings, missed promotions, raises, and benefits in their lifetimes.

✓ Social Security is the only source of income for 25% of women retirees.

✓ More women than men live below the poverty level.

### Ensure Your Own Financial Health with Wealth

Your financial health may not be good right now. After all, you probably don't think about your own welfare—you put your family first. But look at the facts above. It is no wonder many women end up in Medicaid long-term care facilities.

If you are tired of making excuses that let you think you don't NEED to know about money or where to start taking control; or if you were happy to give up financial control when you got married; or if you have no idea how much your family is spending; or if your salary has grown to top even your spouse's; it is not too late do something about it.

**It is time to grow up and take control**. If you want to make sure you do not fit the above profile of women in retirement, you must learn where the family spending goes. Don't assume you will have enough when your spouse or you can no longer work.

**First**, discuss your feelings with your family. **Second**, get to know how your family invests for retirement. **Third**, build a "**Wealth Reserve™**" to make sure you are protected with "assets that grow by themselves" over time. Some members recommend reading *Maxing Out* by Collette Dowling.

As discussed above, your family **Wealth Reserve**™ consists of all the assets you own that "grow by themselves." It allows you to insure and finance yourself instead of giving your hard won income to your broker, banker or agent. Your **Wealth Reserve**™ allows you (and your spouse) to provide for your own permanent life insurance, long-term care insurance, and disability insurance coverage.

Your **Wealth Reserve**™ can provide cash for YOUR retirement funding. If your spouse will receive or does receive a pension, you may be the pension beneficiary. Most pensions provide some fraction of the pre-death benefit to you. However, the amount is usually not enough to ensure that you can continue the same lifestyle as before.

Even if there is a life insurance benefit, at death, a lump sum cannot provide for continued income AND a principal large enough to guarantee your long-term health care needs. Establish and fund your own pension at work or by using a Roth IRA as suggested above. You must make your own financial future.

Your own **Wealth Reserve**™ may allow you to be financially independent like many of our members. With a strategy to meet your specific long term income needs, you can gain the peace of mind that a large growing asset base can provide. The key is taking action immediately. It is TIME not investment skill that creates a **Wealth Reserve**™. You don't need to be genius stock picker. My favorite quote:

"We continue to make more money when snoring than when active."
Warren Buffett, one of the world's best investors

www.berkshirehathaway.com

Our members have shown that they can build that **Wealth Reserve**™ simply by RE-DIRECTING the cash they already spend on financial services they don't need. Financially savvy people buy only the financial products and services they really need. We have shown you how they do it in each of theinsidersguides.com.

Our members have found that they can save up to $3,000 per year using our Insider's Guides. You can't afford to waste that extra $3,000. You can then buy assets that "grow by themselves" Some members put their money in their own business or the stocks of businesses that pay them earnings. That $3,000 becomes $3,202, then $6,811, then $10,877, until they have about $100,000 in 15 years. This is your **Wealth Reserve**™.

# It is NOT too late

Since you may live to be over 80 years of age before you need your **Wealth Reserve**™ for income or health or custodial care, it is not ridiculous to follow our Insider's advice even at age 60. Our members enjoy buying assets that grow without the need to work more hours. They make sure that the $3,000 they saved goes automatically to their business or the accounts they own. If our members work for someone else, they enroll in their employer's retirement plan and some receive a matching amount FREE. If not, they start a Roth IRA.

You may ask, where does the $250 a month ($3,000 a year) come from? It comes from learning about the financial products you really need and buying them directly from quality providers. You may NOT be the spouse responsible for buying insurance and investments. You will probably be the spouse who benefits most by investing the savings in a Roth IRA stock mutual fund.

One member recently moved their mutual funds from Fidelity to Vanguard and saved over $3,000 a year. They were paying about $4,188 or 1.2% of their current account values of $349,000 *each year* for the last 10 years. Now they pay less than 0.20% or $698 per year. Their retirement fund will be $545,000 greater because they pay 0.2% instead of 1.2% per year until retirement. Compare your present mutual fund to a low-cost leader to see how much you are missing:
https://personal.vanguard.com/us/faces/JSP/Funds/Compare/CompareEntryCont ent.jsp?type=etf

# Build your **Wealth Reserve**™

Your **Wealth Reserve**™ consists of all the assets your family owns that "grow by themselves." For your family, that may mean retirement plans, home, rental real estate, securities and mutual funds, and a business, if you own one. Female home ownership is at an all-time high with one-fifth of residential real estate now being held by single females. Women are now the primary breadwinners in roughly one-third of U.S. households.

Financially independent people are independent because they use their income to buy more "assets that grow by themselves." Typically their **Wealth Reserve**™ allows them to feel comfortable because they spend less than they make. If their income were to vanish for five years, they would be able to survive —keeping their family and home intact. Most of our members use their retirement plan for the bulk of their **Wealth Reserve**™. Typically they started investing during their working lives and consistently increased the proportion of their income designated for investments.

Women are more likely to lack a personal pension. Women are more likely to lack the experience to manage the family investments. Women are more likely to inherit assets that they do not know how to grow. Although this situation is changing, it has been my experience that many women need to learn how to control their financial life later than men. Women will have a longer time to make sure their assets will take care of them—producing income far beyond what was originally planned.

Women need to educate themselves NOW about what their family owns and why they own them. Families usually own mutual funds, securities and rental real estate in various taxable, tax-deferred and tax-FREE accounts. Some have left employers with retirement plans after years of accumulation. Most of them have opened IRA rollover accounts and had the new trustee move the money so they continue compounding without receiving it and paying tax. Women need to understand how TAX-FREE or deferred compounding works so they can control the supply of income after their spouse passes on.

Many families have mutual fund accounts at five or more different firms. Some members, especially women, have seen their **Wealth Reserve**™s grow dramatically over the years because they don't buy and sell funds. Some members invest 10% of their income. Most members with sizable accounts started investing early. They saved for their first home down payment, college funds, vacations and cars. Women need to ensure their family has earmarked long-term funding for *their* future financial needs. Increase the amount invested by using our Insider's Guides to cut the commissions and fees on their financial service needs.

## How your **Wealth Reserve**™ saves you up to 40%

Financially savvy members have used our Insider's Guide to Vehicle Insurance to help them save up to $6,000 over 10 years, for instance. Our Insider explains what you need and don't need and why to keep the deductible high. If you are a safe experienced driver, you can benefit by switching to certain insurers. One of them has been rated No. 1 in customer satisfaction for 4 consecutive years by JD Power and pays YOU dividends. Why pay extra commission and subsidize other people's poor driving habits?

Not every member can qualify for every category of savings we explain. However, our Insider provides enough "tricks of the trade" to help almost every member save hundreds of dollars. Members use a Roth IRA to shield their earnings from any taxation. The goal is to have an extra $125,000 tax-FREE when the spouse retires to cover his wife's long-term care needs later on, if any.

Another member from Montclair, NJ used our Insider's Guide to Homeowners Insurance to save $5,000 over 10 years. We explain what you need and don't need and why to keep the deductible high and when **NOT to call your agent or insurer.** We show you where to buy if you have a home "at high risk." If you have never had a claim, you may benefit by switching to a "direct writer." Why subsidize others' claims? In some states, you can save 100% or more by using our Insider's hints.

Another member in Vermont dropped his life insurance after realizing that his adult children did not need the protection any more. Further, after consulting our Insider's Guide to Retirement Spending he determined to invest aggressively to insure that he would have enough to retire when he wanted to. He used our Insider's Guide to Buying Mutual Funds and Securities to save 1% a year on his choice of mutual funds and brokerage firms.

Both members are increasing their **Wealth Reserve**™ with money they did not need to spend on insurance. Members use our Insider's Guide to Vehicle Purchases and will save about $10,000 on their choice of cars. Building your **Wealth Reserve**™ protects you against giving money away to banks, especially the $3,000 to

$4,000 in interest most people pay every year on credit cards and car loans.

Making your money work for 20 years in your **Wealth Reserve**™ can provide about $51,000, enough for a home down payment, car or education. You will have paid only $30,000 ($3,000 for 10 years) for that $51,000. You borrow from your "bank" to pay cash.


## You don't have to make a budget or "tighten your belt."

The **Wealth Reserve**™ strategy works because you don't have to *find* NEW money to build your **Wealth Reserve**™. You use the money you already spend for financial services that you decide you don't need. Instead of buying a car or appliance and paying up to 5 times the price by financing it, you pay cash. However, the cash from your **Wealth Reserve**™ is special. It is "compounded" cash. The $51,000 described above cost you only $30,000! You pay less because you planned ahead. See our <u>Insider's Guide to Banking</u> to avoid paying 5 times the price for large items.

WARNING: This Guide offers a strategy to self-fund your financial needs. This Guide shows you how to drop services you may not need. However, before you change your current accounts, make certain that the alternative plan is in place. Do not close the old account until you have tried the services from your new providers and started your **Wealth Reserve**™.


Typically members are "buy-and-hold" investors. This is what makes women better investors than men. Women are more patient. They know they can't time the market by buying the hot stock or fund. That activity only benefits the brokers and leaves the average investor earning **2.56%** according to a DALBARinc.com study. Some members use Modern Portfolio Theory (<u>riskglossary.com/</u>) to increase returns as they reduce risk. Women members illustrate this strategy in Chapter 2.

Some members have chosen low-cost index funds to keep their **Wealth Reserve**™-building simple. These members believe that broad market indexes provide their best chance of accumulating at 12% annually over the long haul. They don't consider themselves risk-takers but are comfortable leaving 100%

of their long-term money in stock funds. Their short-term goals are accomplished by funding low-cost balanced funds. They used Morningstar.com to screen for the funds they use.

We provided an example of how a **Wealth Reserve**™ works over a lifetime in Chapter 1. Fred and Susan started creating a fund many years ago. They started out just saving for their daughter's college expenses when they got married. They kept using their college fund for more than just college. They used it like a **Wealth Reserve**™ to self-insure and self-fund their lifetime needs. Susan is the investor.

Here are the highlights of the story in which Susan managed her family's financial life.

Fred and Susan had a baby—Natalie—about 35 years ago. They lived in lower Manhattan. Susan worked with one of our Insiders. Susan asked what to do with the money they received from relatives and friends for Natalie's birth. They wanted to protect their new child's future and to have college money. Both Fred and Susan had good insurance benefits at work. Fred and Susan were already aware of the benefits of investing in the pension where the company matched their contributions—like FREE money—and Uncle Sam waits for his.

Fred and Susan picked the stocks with the highest yield and the lowest price. Susan was an underwriter and knew stock values. They agreed on buying stocks because they could buy them directly from the companies and hold them without paying tax on the increased value until they needed the money. Dividends were reinvested and the income tax was not outrageous.

They had $5,000 from gifts and they contributed $6 a day ($350 monthly). By the time Natalie was 18, Fred and Susan had about $300,000. They were temped to stop investing during the 1978 recession, but Susan kept them on track.

They had a car accident and sold stock to pay for the insurance policy deductible. They were saving about $200 a year by taking the $1,000 deductible.

They wanted a house. The cost of the down payment— $15,000—came from Natalie's college fund. They found that most of the $15,000 withdrawal was money they had already paid tax on. They paid the capital gains tax of 20% on about $5,000 of the

$15,000. They avoided the mortgage insurance that because they had a 20% down payment.

They saved on their homeowner's by picking a $5,000 deductible. They saved on credit life, disability, unemployment, and PMI insurance that the mortgage bank tried to add on to their mortgage. All these helped pay for the college fund. For $210 a year, Susan and Fred would have $1,000,000 coverage in case they were sued and needed to pay a lawyer to defend themselves.

They were finally ready for Natalie to go to college. They had $300,000 available for her when she was 18 years old. During this time educational loans were very cheap. So Fred and Susan decided to let the college fund grow—20% to 25% a year—during the 90's. They knew this was unusual because the average gain for Dow stocks was 12% a year. They let the loans grow for the first two years until they could see that they had earned $60,000 for two years straight. So they sold enough stock to pay the loans and the tax of 20% on the stock earnings. Now they realized they did not have to worry about the college loans any more."

Susan told our Insider that they had easily taken care of Natalie's college expense each year from the college fund. They stopped paying for term life insurance policies that she and Fred owned. This saved them another $2,500 a year and they continued to invest the $350 per month.

Susan was disabled within the year. She no longer had disability insurance from work. She was not able to work at all. They decided to cut back on their entertainment, vacation, and hobbies in order to get by on Fred's salary. They also had an emergency expense. They had to sell stock to pay $10,000 for a parent's home repair. The tax on the earnings of the stocks did not push them into the next tax bracket, so they are actually paying much less tax this year anyway. Susan got better and was able to give Natalie a fabulous graduation party and trip to California as a present.

The next year after Natalie graduated, Susan and Fred decided to start their own business. Fred would work part-time. **Susan would work full-time in what she loved**—framing people's pictures. Fred would do the woodwork. Susan would run the store in a charming village nearby. The college fund—now $600,000 or so—gave them the feeling that they would have incomes until they got the store into the black. They didn't need much to pay the store's rent and utilities. The store liability policy was not too bad after Susan picked a higher deductible. Fred's job would provide the health insurance they needed.

The store business allows Fred and Susan to deduct many of the normal expenses associated with their activities. The 'college' fund, no longer for college, allows them to save more on the protection they need for retirement.

They attended a seminar on **long term care insurance** and decided that they can afford it but don't need it. According to page 6 of the Shopper's Guide they received at the seminar, the chance of Fred needing expensive care is 4%; **Susan 13%.** [See our Insider's Guide to Long-term Care Insurance.] If they spent $4,000 a year for up to 30 years, they may never get to use that $120,000 ($2,000 each, times 30 yrs.) because they both are in good health. Anyway, 25% of LTC buyers drop it within two years.

Fred and Susan put the $4,000 in their tax-advantaged retirement plan, connected with their business. This will add another $600,000 for any emergency, including remodeling their home for easy access and hiring a home health aide. These are the most common needs people have, according to the booklet. Worst case, they have assets in a business which helps them with health care.

Fred was still a teacher working part-time and Susan loves the way a picture looks—even bad ones—in a frame.

## Lifestyle Protection

A **Wealth Reserve**™ is usually started when people get motivated to save and invest, usually when they have a child. Every one of our members wishes they had started their **Wealth Reserve**™ or 'self-insurance funds' earlier than they did.

The Reserve Fred and Susan have built up is the *real* **meaning of insurance**: it's lifestyle protection. It is easy to create a **Wealth Reserve**™ or 'Self-Insurance Fund' because the Roth IRA or 401k allows most people to use market securities for their important needs without paying any federal tax on the earnings-- *ever*. The Roth IRA lets you pay for college, home, health, and disabilities without any federal income tax or penalty. Today, members would be able to supplement their pensions with the $900,000 or so they have accumulated without any federal income taxes—Zero, Nothing, FREE.

No matter what your age, a **Wealth Reserve**™ can be created and used because we are all living longer. No person in retirement has ever told me that they have enough. Investing $167 monthly, $2,000 a year, your Reserve can grow to $249,000 to protect your lifestyle in retirement. You can find the $2,000 a year from savings you experience using our Insider's trade secrets. Search each financial product/service you own to squeeze out the money from charges you don't need.

For a woman, a **Wealth Reserve**™ is the security she needs after everyone else in the family has been taken care of. Creating a new life after the loss of your spouse is a whole lot easier when you have a **Wealth Reserve**™.

✓

# 13

## The Insider's Guide for Survivors: Create Your Future Life

✓ You will be able to handle 'executor' details of the estate, and
✓ You will be able to manage the money, and
✓ You will be able to make a new life.

### You can take control and make a new life

1.  The first thing to do is allow yourself the time and space to grieve. You have lost someone dear. Come back to the details in a few days. Don't make decisions about money for 90 days.

2.  Consider the great times. Collect all the pictures and put them in an album so you can visualize the special times together.

3.  I just went through this experience when my Mom died unexpectedly from pancreatic cancer. It happened in a few short months.

Now let's begin. I assume you are the executor of the estate or you are involved in resolving the details of your loved one's passing. You may be working with an attorney or you may have chosen to go it alone. In most states you don't need to have an attorney for small estates under $500,000.

My brother was there at the time of passing. Shortly afterward, he contacted an anatomical gifts registry. My Mom had donated her body for studies. The Registry called the funeral home they use to transport my Mom to the university. They arranged for the obituary she wrote to be printed in the local paper because the local paper refused to take it directly. [Collusion deal?] They charged a fee of $400 to become involved since the Registry had a contract to transport Mom's body. The actual transportation charge of $250 was waived. The Registry website says there is "no charge to the survivors." You should ask the funeral home for a breakdown and explanation of their charges before they get involved. The funeral home ordered the death certificates. Usually ten will be needed for the various bureaus and financial institutions that request it. If there are extensive asset relationships, more may be needed. The funeral home billed $5 each. We never got an explanation for the $400 charge.

The average cost of a funeral in the United States ($6,500) is almost four times that in Great Britain ($1,650) and almost three times what it is in France ($2,200) or Australia ($2,100), according to the national Funeral Consumers Alliance. Some of that difference can be attributed to the cost of the casket. The Funeral Consumers Alliance http://www.funerals.org/ offers tips on making the preparations reasonable in cost. I was lucky in the sense that Mom had already been very specific about the whole funeral and service.

The entire family made a decision about the time and place for the memorial service. My father was recovering from a hospitalization, so my brother went to see him at the recovery center. Mom's death was anticipated. I suggest you have another family member call all the relatives. It is too hard for the immediate family to call and discuss it with every person the deceased knew. The immediate family confirmed the time and place of the memorial service with the church pastor. The time and place were printed in the obituary.

Family members called all of our friends and advisors. These included the family lawyer who had the will. Mom was concerned about Dad's care when she wasn't around and had taken great steps to arrange for Dad to transfer to a continuous care center. She had made some modifications to her will. I had my Dad's power of attorney so I could help him maintain the house and all their other relationships. My Dad had already retrieved their safety deposit box contents from the bank before Mom passed. Unless it is a joint account, your bank may not let you remove the will without documents in some states.

## Executor of an estate

Previous to a meeting of all the family members after the memorial service, I had gone to my parent's town to meet with their lawyer and arrange for the memorial service and meals. How and when you become the executor of an estate is a state decision. I relied on their lawyer to know the procedure. I spent a couple of hours with him as we filed the paperwork needed to begin the probate process, have me take an oath for the probate officer and set up a bank account for the estate. Sometimes this requires that you put up some money to guarantee you will not steal the estate's assets. It may require you to borrow money an existing bank account so the estate can pay expenses. In our case, my parent's joint checking was now my Dad's account (he has the "right of survivorship") and he "loaned" money to the estate account to pay bills like the memorial service expenses.

Depending on what is in the will, the executor basically carries out the instructions in the will. If all the assets are left to the heirs, then your job is basically to use the attorney to help you obtain the cash from the assets, pay the expenses of your loved one's estate and then disburse the remainder and report to the probate court officer. Sometimes trusts are created in the will and you become the trustee.

> A plan will help control your fears

If you were lucky as I was, the assets and expenses and other financial relationships were already known, listed and compiled in an orderly fashion. My Mom was a the family manager and had all the statements of accounts, bills, estimated tax payments and records in one place—in a drawer, labeled in files. I collected all the important papers, jewelry, household items—anything of value—and put them in my car. The house would be closed up and put up for sale after the memorial service.

Whatever expenses were normally paid or shared by the deceased were now expenses of the estate. To make accounting for the probate easier, all the income and expenses should be run through the estate's account. So I paid for the memorial service programs and dinner, obituary publishing, funeral home charges, left over medical bills from final medical treatments, credit card bills, and any expense associated with the house and car (water, electric, phone, cable, insurance, maintenance) she owned, from that account. I paid for my Dad's nursing home and subscriptions and medical bills from their (now his) joint account. I don't have to account for those expenses to probate since the estate does not own that account. I pay only his bills from the 'joint' account. You may be the survivor paying your own bills for the first time. My father sends me bills to pay and I usually look at their check register to confirm that my Mom used to pay them. Dad is not used to paying the bills.

For instance, my parents tithe to their church based upon their two modest pensions and social security income. My Dad wanted to continue as long as he can afford to give. I worked back from what they had been giving to calculate their percentage and then used his bank statements to confirm his income amounts. On the other hand, I called all the organizations that made direct debits of their joint checking to cancel. I sent a change of address form to the post office so all the mail would go to my Dad. He and I sent change of address cards to all his subscriptions since the post office will not continue to forward mail forever. The post office "forgot" and kept delivering to the old address anyway.

The probate process requires that the executor list and value everything that is owned at the time of death. In this way, your state can tax even small estates. (The IRS taxes an estate over $5 million (2011), leaving me to wonder why working people want to cancel the estate tax.) The IRS says:

> Most relatively simple estates (cash, publicly-traded securities, small amounts of other easily-valued assets, and no special deductions or elections, or jointly-held property) with a total value under $5,000,000 (2011) may not require filling. irs.gov/businesses/small/article/0,,id=108143,00.html

Probate can also make sure the heirs get what they were intended to get. I heard a lot of rumors about what Mom had intended for our china and tea set, but she had not written it down with her will. I had spoken with her during the last few months and we discussed this point. She said nothing about any specifics. She was more concerned about taking care of Dad than worrying about who got what. Now that the family has been through the process, I don't think it would have made it easier if she had written down who got what.

# How to distribute the assets in an estate

I had been prepared for this question by reading about being an executor. With the distribution of all the 80 years of stuff in the family home, I had read about ways the stuff can be distributed that keeps the process from tearing a family apart. You may think this method is cold and unfeeling but for our family, it was accepted as the fairest way. The answer for our family—Dad and three grown sons and their wives and kids—was to treat everything as an asset of the estate. Since the assets that could be converted to cash easily would be shared equally by the heirs, everything else would be handled the same way.

For instance, at the family dinner after the memorial service, Dad wanted to give away some books that clearly belonged to Mom, and now to her estate. I explained that since the estate owned everything now (Mom and Dad had agreed to that method in their wills), I would need to account for the gift. A used book has little value so this action was not significant. I explained to the heirs, if Dad started giving away the contents of the house or the car, this would be a problem. Even though Dad helped pay for the car, he did not and never had owned it. And why would the three sons allow him to give it away? What if one of them wanted it? What if I were to believe what one of the wives told me—that Mom had given all our china to one of the (divorced) son's daughter? Should the china belong to the divorced wife's family? Should one son get the car and the other two get nothing?

> An inventory reduces fights

Luckily everyone agreed that having to make an accounting to the probate required us all to be fair with each other. I told the heirs that I had to ignore their hearsay. If one son wanted the car, he must buy it from the estate for the fair market value. The same would apply to the china. In fact, anything of value would have to be accounted for. Obviously, the things that have sentimental value will be the most difficult to split up. However, with a little research on Internet auction sites, it was relatively easy to find the market value of everything of value.

I found the exact match to the lifting-chair, stair-chair, china, flatware, tea set, hutch, dining room table, and chairs online even though some of them were 60 years old. The heirs paid the actual auction or "wholesale" price. My antiques dealer friend confirmed the value of the items. He said that the price he would pay for these items would be 25% to 40% of the price that he or the replacement sites like replacements.com/ would sell them for. Thus a place setting of Mom's china cost $109.95 to replace, but the heir paid only $27.50 for it.

I did an inventory of all the important or valuable items in the house. I priced the ones I found prices for. I asked the heirs to indicate which they were willing to pay for. They did not need to pay the estate yet since they would receive cash from the distribution when it occurred later. I was more concerned with getting the items distributed and the house emptied so we could sell it. The heirs lived 100 miles, 400 miles and 1000 miles away. We had to coordinate everything with a local handyman who actually handled all the clean up and shipping and details. A realtor or local auctioneer could have done these things for us.

Armed with all the family records and papers, I was able to use the lawyer to start the process of identifying and collecting the assets. The lawyer notified Social Security that my Mom would no longer need her checks but that my Dad should receive the death benefit insurance. The Social Security office agreed to visit my Dad in his center, but never showed. The lawyer had already transferred some of my parents' assets to a trust company for convenience. As executor, I had to sign off on forms to retrieve some bonds and notes and mutual funds. However, the assets at a mutual fund in my Mom's name could have stayed there since the trust company only changed the title on the account. For this they charged $1500 or 1% of the assets. This $1500 could have been saved by writing a letter to the mutual fund company instead.

## Work with a lawyer who knows elder law not family law

My experience leads me to conclude that **if** my parents didn't have a family lawyer, I as executor could have done the entire asset gathering on my own without the expense of the lawyer. Lawyers charge 2% to 5% of estate value. He wrote a letter that I needed to sign which needed to be sent back to him which was then sent with the account statement I gave him in the first place. He sent it to the financial institutions that held the assets. The lawyer can only act at the request of the executor—he has no power to order that the account be closed and the check be sent to the estate account. In most cases, I would have been better off doing it myself. It would have saved hundreds of dollars in fees by the lawyer (at $175 plus per hour) and the trust company (1% of assets) and others (whatever grieving families can bear).

However, if you don't have the time, you may want to depend on a lawyer who has been through the process before. Make sure you hire or use someone with experience about elder law. The family lawyer may not have enough experience to do the specific things required by your state. However, an appraiser and antique dealer I know well said that he has done 5 executor processes himself and he feels that if you have the time and patience, it is worth doing yourself. He was gratified by all the help he got from the various bureaus and institutions when he just asked and listened. Nolo.com and ElderLawAnswers.com provide resources.

Finally, when your family situation is known intimately by you, the executor, or you, the one leading the executor, you are the one that must be concerned about assets and benefits no one else knows about. For instance, it turned out that when the lawyer told my Mom's pension record keeper that she had passed on, he did not know that my Dad qualified to receive a death benefit and continue health care supplemental coverage. So he did not start the paperwork needed to receive those benefits.

Luckily, in our family, Mom kept all these certificates of benefits and health care plan statements in one place. In my immediate family, I keep these for my wife in a 3-ring binder so she knows where to go to find them if I am not around. She will find all the numbers she needs and papers showing insurance and benefits owed to her as my survivor. Unfortunately, we never learn this kind of financial stuff in high school. Unless you anticipate your death, you don't think about what your survivor will need to carry on financially. A CD from *Kiplinger* can help: http://store.kiplinger.com/family_records_info.html

Since I had all the records my Mom kept, I went through them to see if there were any current bills to pay. I sent cancellations to all the credit card companies, bank cards, subscriptions my Dad did not want. I sent changes of address to all the places my father did not know about, like the utilities for the house, tax authorities, and local merchants she used. Some of these had been paid automatically from their checking account. Mom had been wise enough to have all their income checks deposited directly into the account. She also saved herself the trouble by having some of the utilities paid directly. I told motor vehicles, the credit bureaus and the post office, she had passed. This will cut down on the chance her identity is stolen by those who do such things for a living.

After sorting through the papers I found at my parents home, I spent two days there making sure every nook and cranny was searched. With the help of my wife and brother, we went through all the drawers and closets and attic and basement. We found unused checks. We marked all the items we were to take out. Most of the valuables were purchased by the heirs so when the auctioneer came to give us an appraisal, he just said 'No thanks.' He explained that it costs a lot to move and auction stuff off. You could hire a clean up crew to take away everything else you don't want. They keep the amount they receive when the sell the items.

A friend of the family called the local charities to take old clothes and some items. Dad took all the clothes and books and pictures he wanted to the nursing home. The handyman volunteered to clean out the house and sell whatever was left. Basically these items were gifts to him. None of us needed the bedroom sets, end tables, lamps, sofas, chairs, desks and bookcases.

As the eldest son, I felt it was my pleasure to be executor for my Mom. I was glad to make sure Dad was taken care of since that was my Mom's greatest concern at the end. My job was difficult because it hurts to have to review all the things that reflected 60 years of their lives. My Dad did what he could but the job is too big to handle alone. It is almost better to have someone else just throw everything away after the family has picked out the obvious mementos. My Mom had kept extensive journals and teaching materials and lesson plans from her many activities that I did not know about. I will take my time in reading them. I guess it is NOT better to have someone toss everything. Our family pictures were scanned and collected in albums for my Dad to keep with him. We can all enjoy the pictures for many years to come via email and CD and DVD show.

# Gathering the assets of the estate

My Mom had different types of accounts. She had a small life insurance policy, IRA, regular mutual fund accounts, savings' notes (certificates of deposit), checking account, and spousal health coverage from her former job. Social Security also provides a small life insurance benefit which you can't collect easily. They insist on my Dad (in a nursing home) standing in line in *their* offices. For each type of account, I had to contact the institution and ask the procedure for claiming the benefit. Your lawyer would have to do the same since every process is different.

✓　If your loved one left a deferred annuity, a non-spouse beneficiary may have to pay <u>federal income taxes</u> on the gain. Even small estates may have tax to pay.*
✓　If they left mutual funds, securities, or other assets that have gone up in value, the beneficiary will **NOT** have to pay <u>income taxes</u> on the gains.  The estate may have tax to pay.*
✓　Life insurance can provide a legacy at death without income taxes. The estate may have tax to pay.*

*Estate value is assets less debts at death. The portion not taxed by the feds <u>changes</u> annually. <u>IRS.gov</u> Every state has its own rates and processes:  <u>bankrate.com/brm/news/news_taxes_home.asp</u> The life insurance claim form required a copy of the death certificate. If you find premium payments for life insurance, but don't know which insurance company, you can use the MIB's Policy Locator database with 170 million records. You or your attorney can trace life policies to the correct insurance company. Policy Locator provides you with the insurance company to which the decedent applied for coverage. Cost of a search is $75 at <u>www.policylocator.com</u>.
　　　　The IRA account at a big mutual fund firm required that I compose a letter with the vital statistics of the heirs on it. Each heir had to take the form to their local bank for a 'signature guarantee' by a bank officer. Another form required notary signature identification. Another required the death certificate which they kindly returned after making a copy. The mutual fund firms required their form and a death certificate and an account number

to transfer the money into. The trust company already had the instructions from me, the executor, to transfer money to the heirs' mutual fund accounts. They could receive a check instead.

Again, I was lucky because there were enough different assets in different places that I could direct to the estate checking account to pay expenses immediately, while others would go to the heirs after the estate filed a form with the probate. My Mom had done the correct type of planning in advance. She had titled and invested some assets so that she controlled them if they were needed but would pass on to heirs at a stepped-up basis without income tax due. nolo.com/definition.cfm.

Mom owned the family car. Her will directed it be sold immediately. My brother found out online that this car was worth about $12,000. Luckily, the wife of an heir wanted the car and made the purchase from the estate. I had to sign the title and provide a Certificate of Appointment from the county clerk with raised seal to the buyer. She paid the estate account with a check for the records.

To sell the house, I contacted three real estate brokers in the area. My father had recommended one he knew and had used in the past. He provided a very low guess as to the value of the home. I picked three unknown brokers based on comparable homes they were selling. I used the Internet (realtor.com) to obtain their name and number. I interviewed them in person on my next visit to the house to clean up.

I told them what I felt were the most important benefits of the house. The house was on a *cul de sac* and bordered a wide creek overlooking a large tract of trees. It had a fantastic view from a covered patio that extended across the front of the house. Dad had a full bench swing hanging from the ceiling. Deer and ducks came by during the night and day. I asked them to explain how they would market the house and who would be the best buyer. I decided against the one who brought the wrong types of comparable houses they had sold (comps) to illustrate how they could sell. I picked the one who sounded like they understood how to find that special buyer. They agreed with me that the others had priced the house very low. They suggested putting out an asking price that was 30% higher than what the others quoted.

I signed the contract by fax after having the local family lawyer check it. The realtor made several showings over the next month while the heirs were having things picked up or discarded. I don't think more that 10 people saw the house. The broker was going on vacation and did not plan to have an open house until 2 months after the listing. I was not happy with this but left it to the broker.

Suddenly, just one month after engaging the broker, I had the buyer. They had seen the house and wanted the view. The home itself was nothing special. The buyer was bidding against another offer that came in on the same Monday. The buyer did not need to get a mortgage. They matched the competing bidder's price almost immediately and within a half hour we had a deal. The price was 31% over the original family real estate broker's estimate. It was also above what I had told the broker I was expecting after negotiating down from the asking price. (I had not taken the first very low bid. I did give them a chance to outbid the final buyer's bid.) The buyer wanted the house in 3 weeks after inspections. I agreed. I told the local attorney to have the closing without me. I would UPS my signature. Obviously the heirs and my Dad were thrilled. I suspected the first broker had not considered how important it was to sell the property's strength—the view. Lesson: Always get at least 3 opinions—especially if you don't live there.

Finally, after identifying or obtaining the value of all the assets of the estate, I was ready to complete and sign the Appraisement of the Estate. This document tells the probate what kinds and amounts of assets are in the estate—home $100,000, securities $65,000, etc—and who the heirs are. It does not require an inventory of the household goods because the value is under a certain amount in some states. The heirs sign a document saying they are satisfied with the allocation of the goods. These documents are filed with probate. I discovered in this process that **you may never have to probate a will** if you title the assets correctly and have no children. For instance, pay on death--POD and survivor accounts, pensions, annuities and IRAs are **not probated** if they have a beneficiary designated. A **will is useful to designate your executor and custodian** of your children. In many states, some judge decides whether the surviving parent can remain the child's parent. Some system?

# Types of assets in an estate

You can transfer many kinds of assets to your family before or after death. One of the members of our Network had an adequate pension and supplemental income so that she could buy a single payment life insurance policy for $50,000. The benefit of about $150,000 would be split equally to her four grandchildren as her legacy. She did this outside of her will and probate. The grandchildren or their guardians will have access to the funds within 30 days. She does not have a big estate so the policy will not create an estate tax problem.

Another method of accomplishing a legacy is the way members John and Liz did. Investing $100,000 in a low-cost tax-managed mutual fund for 15 years may mean leaving $600,000 (at market average of 12% a year) to the children. At death the exact value is distributed according to the survivor's will. If their estate totals less than the federal exemption, the $600,000 is passed with no estate tax. The benefit of this method is that John and Liz can use the assets for long-term care, if needed, **and** the heirs will pay no federal income tax.

Hopefully your loved one did not leave a deferred annuity untapped. They paid no tax on the earnings so the named beneficiaries must pay income tax at the beneficiaries' rates. Even though the annuity may have grown to a sizable amount, the legacy could be much less than thought. If the annuity had been "annuitized" before death, monthly income from the annuity could have been used to buy life insurance or a growth mutual fund inside a Roth IRA for benefits that are totally tax-FREE. An accountant needs to define how best for the beneficiaries to take the money now. If the spouse inherits, the annuity can be continued.

An IRA left to any person other than the spouse may have tax problems. If you are the surviving spouse, you can use it like your own IRA--pay tax when you withdraw funds. If the deceased left it to their estate or other non-person, the taxes on the gain must be paid over a 5 year period. If the named beneficiary is a person, there are several options, including stretching the payout over many years. irs.gov/publications/p590/ch01.html#d0e5724

If you are the non-spouse beneficiary, you can liquidate the

IRA. Tax is due as if it was a paycheck to you. The primary beneficiary could choose to disclaim, or give up control of, the IRA while the estate is being settled. The account would then pass to the contingent beneficiary or the estate. See a trained IRA advisor or read Ed Slott's *Your Complete Retirement Planning Road Map*. irahelp.com/

Leaving an unused IRA (mandated withdrawals at 70.5 years) makes the IRS's mouth water. The IRS can assess a 50 percent penalty on the amount that should already have been taken out. There are taxes to pay also. Finally, the amount that the designated beneficiary is required to withdraw from an inherited IRA can vary so check with your tax person. irahelp.com/

If your loved one's estate value will exceed the exemption, hopefully they made a plan that lowers their estate value by changing the ownership of the assets or giving them to their family before death. One member had a large insurance policy death benefit (not cash value) which would have put his estate over the exemption. The member transferred 'ownership' of the policy to his four adult children. Each offspring cannot sell the policy by themselves and their share of the death benefit does not put them close to their own exemption limit if they should die first. The member continues to pay the premium. Each child will receive 1/4 of the death benefit. IRS.gov

## How much could have been transferred?

Your loved one could have transferred as much as their plan designated for estate tax and beneficiary income tax purposes. The calculations and timing become complicated. Certain assets that have grown in value pass to beneficiaries without federal income tax due. These include life insurance death benefits, real property, securities, and personal property, as long as you don't sell them previously. Other account assets with tax-deferral benefits like IRAs, annuities, and pensions pass with the same taxation as ordinary income. All may be included in the estate and taxed at up to 46%. The estate consists of all the assets owned by your loved one at death. A little planning avoids all estate taxes. The political frenzy of some commentators about the "death" tax seems to be contrived.

In our situation, my Mom had planned ahead so that my parent's biggest assets were in her name at death. This allowed the heirs to receive the cash without any income taxes being due. And, in most cases, because of good planning, the assets could be passed to the family without the possibility of the assets being confiscated by creditors. I had my Dad's power of attorney.

Before making plans for a legacy, they made sure they did not need supplemental retirement income or emergency health care funds. A strategy that provides for both contingencies is the one that grows assets at low taxation and is distributed to the heirs without income tax to them. If the funds are needed for an emergency, they are readily available. The tax-managed growth funds used by our members do this efficiently and at low cost. Historically, the funds compound at 10% over periods greater than 10 years.

WARNING: This Guide offers suggestions on how to manage your legacy yourself. This Guide suggests how to establish a plan to manage your family legacy for your family needs. Before you change your current accounts, make certain that the alternative plan is in place. Do not cancel any accounts before you check with your lawyer about your alternative arrangement. Start your **Wealth Reserve**™ to guarantee your future independence.

Finally, all the assets had been converted into cash or sold to heirs or others for cash. All expenses that I knew about were paid. At the time of my appointment as executor, the lawyer arranged for another lawyer to publish my Mom's death as a Notice to Creditors for a $75 fee. This allows me to close the estate in months not years. A creditor is out of luck after I close it and distribute the remainder of assets in most states.

The final distribution of assets and accounting to the probate take place in different ways depending on local custom. I was lucky in that the heirs split the balance of the estate without getting angry and suing each other and me. The estate may have a number of tax returns to be done. In my case, my Dad and Mom had income in the year of her death. I had to get the returns done.

Your state may tie their estate tax to the federal one, so no state estate tax may be due because the federal exemption. Check with your tax person about what needs to be filed when. Large estates need to pay the Feds in nine months, no matter how long it takes to sell or mortgage the deceased's business or assets.

The final chapter in your loved one's life never really ends. They live on in your memory. In my case, Mom's life will never be over because her husband, sons, grandchildren, relatives, and friends will remember her by the things she did for them and others. For instance, one son's divorced wife will never forget the way she was supported as a new wife and mother. She wrote a beautiful memorial to my Mom on Mom's church website. In part she said:

*I can't begin to tell you what she meant to me as a mother-in-"love" as a mentor, and as a grandmother to my amazing and beautiful daughter. When I look at [her] I realize that without [Mom] I wouldn't have the greatest gift I've ever received.*

## Now you are on your own

When the estate is closed, your new financial life begins. Now you must learn to handle not only your inheritance but perhaps your new financial responsibilities. Part of the reason I am sharing my personal experiences of this loss and transition is that I know it can be devastating. I was lucky that I had some training in how to handle money matters. I have made it my mission to help others who want to take charge of their financial lives but don't know how. Before and after I worked in financial services, I was misled by people in the industry so I am motivated to NOT let it happen to you. I know sales people are trying to make a living but that is no excuse for incomplete advice in my mind. I hope that you will be your own person and have control over your money and make your own decisions. Beware of those who bring you solutions without alternatives you can understand and afford long term.

## What to avoid .

✓ Letting others decide for you. Take control of your own future.
✓ Banks, agents, and brokers have targeted the $ billions to be inherited by us.
✓ Not making a comprehensive financial plan for all your assets.

**Avoid buying financial products without a plan** of what you want to accomplish with your money. Sales people practice all their lives to give you a reason to buy *their* favorite product NOW. It is like going to the convenience store—you will buy anything on impulse. No one likes to admit they made a mistake. It is hard to get your money back. Don't buy anything until you complete your plan.

Every banker, agent, broker and scam artist knows the game—meet with the folks with the money: us. All financial firms are pushing annuities today. Guess what? Sellers receive 14% or more (bankrate.com) of the deposit in exchange for a promise that you can earn a higher return than a CD without current taxes. If you don't need the money now, a fixed rate annuity probably sounds good. But, you can't get your money back easily and as rates climb, your rate will lag the current rate. The problem is that your heirs will have to pay the income tax on the gains of the annuity. There are better ways to avoid taxes. See our Insider's Guide to Wealth Transfer.

A financial plan helps you make sure your money does what you want it to do. A sales person is not trained to give you the low-cost alternatives. For 20 years, our Insider worked with sales people in a Wall Street securities firm and banks. He found that brokers and bankers concentrate on selling the three or four products that the firm determined benefits it. Our Insider noted that the sales people do not sell the best product for your situation or even the products with the lowest costs to you, the buyer. They sell what fits

> **$100 INVESTED NOW IS WORTH $10,000 IN THE FUTURE**

the firm's sales strategy. It is like going to your local hardware store to buy a gas grill when the same grill is available at 50% off at the "big box" stores. You lose. You could have a barbeque with an original Weber. You could pay $500 or $250. Remember, that $250 is worth $25,000 in time.

Plans are easy to make and they don't require a professional to succeed. We show you how to buy "assets that grow by themselves." This Guide boils down most advisors' plans to three steps that you can prepare in one hour. It helps you stay on target. A 15-minute quarterly review is all you need to be sure your future is on target. You are in control and you know exactly where you stand on the road to your goals. Consolidating various mutual funds with similar objectives—short-term growth and income or long-term accumulation—may save you over $3,000 a year in fees. Diversification means holding many types of assets not holding many mutual funds. Many members find one balanced and one US stock and one international stock fund enough.

Once you know what type of assets you will inherit, you can begin to plan how you will use them. As a survivor, you will need to learn how to become financially independent. Our members use three steps: 1) Set goals, 2) Attach timelines to them, and 3) Buy the right low-cost financial products to fit the need. Independents don't overspend for things they don't need. They keep it simple because a simple plan is easy to follow and maintain. Success in becoming independent is 90% patience not intricate and expensive maneuvering. They use the Insiders Guides to save on each product and service they need.

## Best value

✓ "Direct" providers don't have the expenses of brokers, agents and fancy buildings.
✓ Products with total expenses under 0.30% with no surrender, commissions, annual fees, loads.
✓ Best products grow tax-advantaged now and pass tax-free at death.

The best value is usually a quality product without the annual fees or commissions or surrender charges or loads or sales pressure from using a sales person. Using the information in this Guide, you can buy DIRECT from the top rated financial providers just like the professionals do. The money you save and invest year after year can enhance your legacy considerably.

Just as important, you control the future of your financial life. With our Guides you have more alternatives that benefit you not the sales person. You gain peace of mind from understanding how to use your funds to accomplish your goals for current expenses and your legacy. Tax-managed mutual funds from Vanguard or T. Rowe Price have low annual fees and no commissions.

One member has a will that passes the assets to family heirs with no income taxes due at death. Beneficiaries can use all the assets for any purpose—without having to pay income taxes on the gains. They can build their own **Wealth Reserve**™. See how $200 a month can grow below.

Using your inheritance to grow your **Wealth Reserve**™ allows you to have the assurance that you can save on the insurance you need (self-insure) and large purchases you need (self-fund). We gave examples of this activity in the chapters above.

Notice from the chart below how this approach can enlarge your **Wealth Reserve**™ over time. By buying "assets that grow by themselves" with your savings from lower premiums, fees and finance charges, you can become independent financially. You may be able to finally do some of the things you thought were not possible before. One member opened a picture framing business this way. Add your inheritance to your reserve and it becomes huge.


## How assets build your **Wealth Reserve**™

Of course, if you are already in retirement, you may need your **Wealth Reserve**™ to supplement your retirement income. If your loved one's pension and social security are no longer income for you, the inheritance could provide a 4%-6% income for life. You need to remember that inflation robs your funds of their buying power every year. Investing in bonds or CDs that pay 5% will not let your **Wealth Reserve**™ grow if inflation and your withdrawal rate are 4%-6%. Our Insider's Guide to Retirement Spending above may help you plan your spending.

On the other hand, if you have enough assets for your current lifestyle, you can plan how to use them for your new interests and your legacy. One member wanted to make sure

> A member bought a 20 payment whole life insurance policy so that her church received a sizable gift whenever she passes. SBLI whole life insurance is among the most competitively priced in the industry. The member liked the history of SBLI as a low-cost provider of insurance to working people.

she had enough for long-term care later, if needed, and a legacy tax-FREE to her children. She purchased a low-cost total stock index mutual fund that averaged 12% per year over periods longer than 10 years. The index does not buy and sell so it requires few taxes now.

A widowed member with 5 grandchildren wished to provide each with a gift at her death. She was wealthy and the life insurance death benefit would have increased the estate tax bill. She purchased a single payment policy making her 2 sons the owners and their kids the beneficiaries. Her estate will not have to pay tax on the face amount and her grandchildren will share the $1,000,000 tax-free death benefit.

You can review how to transfer your inheritance to your family in our The Insider's Guide to Wealth Transfer above. You can buy tax-managed/efficient funds. $10,000 becomes $25,000 in 10 years at 10%. The funds grow with little current tax and low expenses. Your Will designates heirs who pay no income tax. If you need the funds, the gains are taxed at lower rates. Whole life insurance creates an immediate legacy. At age 60, a $25,000 legacy costs about $33 per month. At age 75, a $20,000 legacy costs about $165 per month. Single payment or modified whole life buys the benefit with one payment. At age 65, a female non-smoker can buy about $66,000 in death benefits for about $20,000 without fluid tests.

Trusts are designed to fit specific needs to transfer wealth and control taxation. Living in your home after giving it away or making a reverse mortgage for more income are options. Giving away property now that has increased in value can provide tax deductions and an income for life.

Your time horizon determines your choice of financial instruments. If your life expectancy is more than 10 years, you can maintain control of your assets for emergencies and, at the same time, grow your legacy for your family using tax-managed funds. You pay little income tax now as your tax-managed mutual funds grow. Your family pays NO income tax when the funds are bequeathed to them in your will.

If you want to provide a living gift to your grandchildren now, you can contribute $13,000 per year to their 529 college fund. You can give any number of people $13,000 (2011) or less each year without jeopardizing your estate tax exemption. Use our

Insider's Guide to Education Funding to save up to $20,000 in account fees.

You can make annual gifts of up to $5,000 (2009) to a young person's Roth IRA. They will have a tax-**FREE** fund of $1 million at age 65. They must have matching income amounts from any source to be eligible. Check chapter 2 of IRS.gov Pub 590 for complete rules for a Roth IRA.

Another strategy is to buy one life insurance policy for all your named beneficiaries outside your will and probate. You can add or subtract names to the list. You can purchase the policy with one payment or periodic payments for the rest of your life.

Deferred annuities offer you, NOT your heirs, the benefits of tax-deferred growth. Unfortunately, your heirs get a big tax bill if you don't begin using these annuities before your will is read. Deferred annuities should be annuitized and the periodic payments used to buy a tax-**FREE** legacy for your family. You can also give them to a charity for a current deduction and income to buy a tax-FREE legacy.


# The critical elements

1. Select a company with high financial strength and experience with the product.
2. Make sure the product's strengths and weaknesses fit your plan.
3. Balance inflation risk with market risk. The annual fees rob you of the power of compounding.
4. Know the salesperson, if you don't buy direct. Check the finra.org/ (800.289.9999) and insurance department (NAIC.org).
5. Confirm your understanding of the annual fees and commissions you will pay in writing.


# Chart your financial future

✓ Your union or association or mutual fund firm may offer fee-based planning services at low cost. wiserwomen.org/pdf_files/dontrun.pdf

✓ You can complete your financial plan. Chapter 2 shows you how to buy "assets that grow by themselves." It assures you will accomplish your goals from Chapter 1.

✓ Find a Fee-only Planner if you need help: NAPFA.org. Learn more: http://ocw.uci.edu/courses/course.aspx?id=12

Seek a fee-only planner if you don't feel confident you can gain control of your financial life using our TheInsidersGuides.com. A financial plan needs to be revised AFTER retirement or income loss in order to make sure you have enough income for the rest of your life. Many people are living to age 90 or more and need an income for 30 years. Since inflation of 3% cuts the purchasing power of income by 50% in 25 years, we need to plan how funds are invested to keep pace with our needs. Check our Insider's Guide to Buying an Annuity above to see why this "darling" of the industry **may not be right for you**. There are alternatives.

In a real sense, we all need to keep our investment plan working AFTER retirement begins. Many independent people keep about half of our assets in stock funds through retirement so that they can maintain the same income purchasing power that they had when they began retirement. Many people keep working past 65 in order to supplement their declining income.

Since we don't know how long we will need an income in retirement, we need to plan for both--income to live on for perhaps 30 years or more and a legacy for our family's benefit without taxes. You can use our Insider's Guide to Retirement Spending above to make sure you have enough. Once you have done that, you can relax.

Many financial advisors claim to provide the expertise to manage your portfolio for life. However, there are no guarantees (except the fees). Things happen. Even if you are wealthy, an illness or accident can severely curtail your ability to retain enough assets to live at the same standard for life and leave a legacy too. See our Insider's Guide to Long-term Care Insurance above. The best each of us can do is to make a plan we understand so we stick with it.

## A legacy can be created in many ways:

1. Financial assets in a taxable account. Heir pays no income tax. Value is 'stepped-up.' nolo.com/index.cfm
2. Financial assets in a tax-deferred account. Heir pays income tax.
3. Financial assets in a Roth IRA account. Heir pays no income tax.
4. Financial assets in an insurance policy. Heir pays no income tax.
5. Financial assets in a trust. Heir pays no income tax. Trust does.

## Stock mutual funds work the hardest for you and your heirs

1. Tax-managed and growth index mutual funds grow with little current taxation.
2. Index funds usually have lower expenses since they buy and hold market securities.
3. The size of your legacy depends on time not on what you buy. Since 1976, Vanguard's 500 Index has averaged over 12% per year ended 2007.
4. Taxes on the accumulation of value are payable only if you sell the funds. Tax on the gains is at a more favorable rate. There are NO INCOME TAXES due when passed to your heirs. Designate "Payable on Death" beneficiary to avoid probate.
5. Funds accumulated inside a Roth IRA for 5 years are tax-FREE.
6. Funds without beneficiary are subject to estate tax and the probate process.

## Annuities, IRAs and Pensions

1. There is a maximum contribution, mandatory distribution, income tax payable by your heirs.
2. There are surrender charges, fees, mortality expenses, commissions.
3. There are no medical questions, blood tests, doctor statements, MIB.com reports.

4. Subject to estate tax but not subject to probate process.

# Life Insurance

1. There is a maximum contribution, no mandatory distribution, no income tax payable by your heirs.
2. There are surrender charges, annual fees, mortality expenses, commissions.
3. There are medical questions, blood tests, doctor statements, MIB.com reports.
4. Subject to estate tax but not subject to probate process. Check for an unclaimed policy at MIB.com.

# Trust assets

1. There is no maximum contribution, no mandatory distribution, and no income tax payable by your heirs.
2. There are initial costs and annual fees.
3. Trust pays income taxes but not subject to probate process.

***Long-term investment funds let you keep control of your assets and leave a legacy FREE of income tax to your heirs.***

# Your Retirement Spending Checklist

1. Keep 18 months of expenses in a low-cost short-term bond or money market fund (Vanguard.com) with check-writing. https://personal.vanguard.com/us/funds/snapshot? FundId=0039&FundIntExt=INT
2. Pay down all debt. Even if your mortgage provides a tax deduction, you have better uses for your income.
3. Keep sufficient auto, home, lawsuit, and health insurance to avoid catastrophic expenses. Use our Insider's Guides on each product to save up to $3,000 annually. For instance, members use a **Wealth Reserve**™ for life, disability and LTC insurance in retirement.
4. Draw down the required amounts of your tax-deferred plans: pensions, 401K, IRA, SEP, and Social Security. There are penalties

for not withdrawing the correct amount.

5.  Sell assets that have lost ground to offset gains first; then long-term taxable, then tax-deferred account assets, finally tax-free. Sell assets to re-balance your overall asset allocation.

6.  If you have sufficient income in retirement, arrange to transfer assets to family members so that they do not have to pay your income or estate taxes upon death. Use our Insider's Guide to Wealth Transfer above to pass assets without taxes due. Deferred annuities pass to family with income tax owed at the beneficiaries' rates. Our Insider says that 94% of annuity buyers never use their annuity for income. They pass it to family members who are taxed at higher rates.

7.  Establish a small business to do the things you like to do. Your expenses can be deductible from your income and your family gains benefits not available to most retirees. If you need health insurance supplements, educational experiences, travel, transportation, liability insurance, and other lifestyle needs, your business can help provide them.

8.  Create and fund your buy/sell business succession plan to avoid dissolution and unequal legacy assets.

9.  An income annuity will provide a monthly income for life. But you can lose money if interest rates are low when you buy it. It is better to ask your mutual fund family to move a monthly amount into your bank without any annuity fees. You save thousands of dollars in fees and lost interest.

10. Keep investing in stock mutual funds after retirement. You and your heirs pay no income taxes if you use a Roth IRA.

11. Confirm that your assets will not exceed the current federal and state estate tax exemption amount. If they might at your death, you can avoid the tax by changing the owner of the assets. A complex estate requires a competent estate attorney.

irs.gov/publications/p553/

# Asset Value over Time

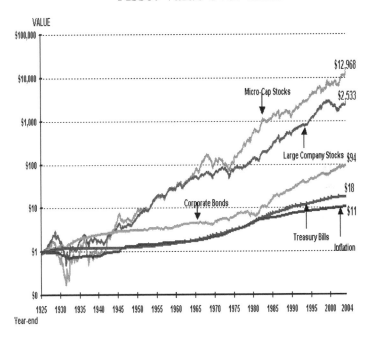

# There are many ways to control assets. Consult an attorney

**Joint tenant with survivorship**
Assets passed to the 'survivor'
Assets passed at death FREE of income tax
Avoids probate

**Tenant by entirety**
Assets passed to the spouse not creditors
Assets passed at death FREE of income tax
Avoids probate

**Tenants in common**
Asset share passed by owner's will
Assets passed at death FREE of income tax
Probate according to owner's state

**Community property**
Assets acquired by either belong to both
Assets passed at death to beneficiary of will
Probate according to owner's state
Assets before marriage need protection

**Revocable living trust**
Give property to trust
You are trustee
Third party guidance
Trust buys future assets
Avoids probate
Controls businesses
Keep assets private
Legacy simplified
Initial cost to transfer
Annual costs
Tax same as individual

**Charitable trusts**
Avoid income, gains, and estate taxes
Asset cannot be reclaimed
Income for life arrangement

**Durable power of attorney**
Person acts for you when you can't
Accident victim
Incompetence

**Accounts for others**
Living trust
Assets passed at death FREE of income tax
Avoids probate

**Family limited partnership**
Assets shifted to children
Tax on accumulation reduced
Assets control retained
Buy/sell agreement for liquidation

**Other strategies**
Family-owned life insurance
Business-owned life insurance
Business-owned assets
Limited liability companies
Gifting assets Your Foundation (DAF) vanguardcharitable.org/

# Conclusion

The best alternative to buying a LTC policy is to self-insure your retirement needs. Having assets to meet your needs no matter what happens is great. An income or immediate annuity purchased with part of your retirement dollars as part of your Retirement Spending budget can help you control your spending. You maintain your purchasing power. It is a curious factor in working with wealthy people: the more they have the more likely they use a budget to help them maintain their wealth. Those that don't need it, use it and those that need it, avoid it.

I hope that you will follow my suggestion to make an investment plan and stick with it. A plan will help you avoid losing your nest egg early. The plan helps maintain it for 30+ years. When others lose their heads in the market, you have a guideline to follow. It helps remind you of your goals in retirement. There are reasons for doing what you do.

I consider the tax-FREE **Wealth Reserve**™ as a new American Retirement System. It provides growth and income without federal taxes. You can build one and convert your IRA to a Roth IRA. You have eliminated taxes on part of your income in the future. Since I assume taxes will be higher later, this strategy beats others.

The essence of this system is a self-directed tax-FREE fund you can use to self-insure and self-fund your financial needs. This eliminates taxes on accumulations, interest paid on loans, premiums wasted on bogus coverage, and false peace of mind.

Take advantage of the miracle of compounding. Security is achieved by having money. Assets that "grow by themselves" provide the wealth to those who are patient. You are assured that your nest egg will continue to grow faster than inflation. You won't have to give away hard-earned cash to insure events that are very improbable. You have a strategy to deal with all the risks of modern life on the assumption that not all negative events will occur to you at the same time. You are insured for the rest.

You will know from where your future income will come. Employer pensions and government support are becoming extinct. You can control your assets without giving up a large chunk to the ever present "middleman"--sales people. In the 21st century, you can create a guaranteed income **plus** build your **Wealth Reserve**™.

# Resources

Compounding
Moneychimp.com/calculator/compound_interest_calculator.htmr
Amateur stock pickers not sellers Aaii.com/
Mutual fund costs Sec.gov/answers/mffees.htm
Mutual fund fees Sec.gov/investor/tools/mfcc/mfcc-int.htm
Mutual fund investing Sec.gov/answers/mutfund.htm
Government studies http://www.cbo.gov/
MF, ETF, Stock information Finance.yahoo.com/
Details on Rothira.com/
Details on Roth 401k Bankrate.com/brm/news/sav/20050518a1.asp
Details on Irahelp.com/
Glossary Investorwords.com/
Greatest investor Buffett's comments: Berkshirehathaway.com/

## Theinsidersguides.com   You can save up to . . .

| | |
|---|---|
| Vehicle Insurance | $6,000 over 10 years |
| Homeowner's Insurance | $2,000 over 10 years |
| Life Insurance | $20,000 over 20 years |
| Lawsuit Insurance | $3,000 over 10 years |
| Health Insurance | $5,000 over 10 years |
| Disability Insurance | $5,000 over 10 years |
| Long Term Care | $40,000 over 20 years |
| Education Funding | $20,000 over 18 years |
| Retirement Spending | $1,000s over 30 years |
| Banking | $3,000 each year |
| Annuities | $20,000 in 20 years |
| Mutual Funds/Securities | $3,000 each year |
| Spending Plan | Reach every goal |
| Vehicle Purchase | $10,000 per vehicle |
| Mortgage Purchase | $3,000 per contract |
| **Wealth Reserve**™ | $1,000,000 |
| Wealth Transfer | $20,000 in 10 years |
| What NOT to buy | 101 products to avoid |
| Living Insurance | $120,000 over 20 years |
| Survivors | It is your life now |
| Self-insurance | $20,000 over 20 years |
| Self-Funded 'bank" | $125,000 in 15 years |
| Business | $30,000 in 10 years |
| Women | It is your life to live |

# Learn to invest; not speculate

*The **Millionaire Next Door**: The Surprising Secrets of America's Wealthy,* Thomas Stanley, William Danko

*The **Wealthy Barber**,* David Chilton

*Common Sense on Mutual Funds: New Imperatives for the **Intelligent Investor**,* John C Bogle

*A **Random Walk** Down Wall Street,* Burton Malkiel.

*Stocks for the Long Run: The Definitive Guide to Financial Market Returns and **Long-Term Investment Strategies**,* Jeremy J. Siegel, Donald G. Coxe

***Everything You've Heard About Investing is Wrong!**,* William Gross

***Psychology** and the Stock Market,* David Dreman

*Fooled by **Randomness**,* Nassim Teleb

*Against the Gods: The Remarkable **Story of Risk**,* Peter L Bernstein

*Winning with Index Mutual Funds: **How to beat Wall Street** at its own game,* Jerry Tweddell & Jack Pierce

*The Only Guide to a **Winning Investment Strategy** You'll Ever Need,* Larry Swedroe

***One Up on Wall Street**,* Peter Lynch

***Ordinary People**, Extraordinary Wealth,* Ric Edelman

*The Intelligent **Investor**,* Benjamin Graham, Warren E. Buffett (Preface)

*Eight Steps to **Seven Figures**,* Charles B. Carlson

***Bogle** on Mutual Funds,* John C. Bogle

***Earn More** (Sleep Better): The Index Fund Solution,* Richard E. Evans

*Perfectly Legal: The Secret Campaign to **Rig Our Tax System** to Benefit the Super–Rich - and Cheat Everybody Else,* David Cay Johnston

*Maximize **Your IRA**,* Neil Downing

*Index Your Way to **Investment Success**,* Walter R. Good, Roy W. Hermansen

***Tricks** of the Trade: An Insider's Guide to Using a **Stockbroker**,* Mark Dempsey

*Mobius on **Emerging Markets**,* Mark Mobius

*25 **Myths You've Got to Avoid**-- If You Want to Manage Your Money Right: The New Rules for Financial Success,* Jonathan Clements

***Investment Policy: How to Win the Loser's Game**,* Charles D. Ellis

***Wealth Without Wall Street**: Buy Direct -- Avoid the Commissions, Fees, Loads,* Dan Keppel

*The **Simple Financial Life**: How to get what you want without going into debt and living paycheck to paycheck,* Dan Keppel

***Build Wealth Without Extra Money or Time**: You don't need to budget or get an extra job,* Dan Keppel

# The Author

Dan Keppel has been helping people find financial services that fit their lifestyles since working in a securities firm, an insurer, two banks and his own MoneyCoach service. His book, *The Insiders' Guides to Buying Discount Financial Services: Buy Direct and Save $3,000 Every Year,* shows you how, what and where to buy financial products like industry insiders do—directly from the highest rated companies for less. He edits TheInsidersGuides.com and was an adjunct at a local college. He lives in Montclair, NJ with his wife, daughter and two cats, Anu and Katze.

He recently lost his Dad who he helped navigate years in two nursing homes.

Made in the USA
Lexington, KY
16 April 2016